Fanny Bienenfeld Lust

REMEMBERING REGINA

My Journey to Freedom

To: Joe;
Lest We Forget!

Fanny Lust

Fanny Bienenfeld Lust

REMEMBERING REGINA

My Journey to Freedom

Yad Vashem ★ Jerusalem
The International Institute for Holocaust Research

Fanny Bienenfeld Lust
Remembering Regina

Academic Editor: Bella Gutterman
Language Editor: Rifkah Goldberg
Production Editor: Ita Shapiro Haber
Hebrew Texts Translation: Naftali Greenwood

ISBN 978-965-308-486-5

Typesetting: PageUp

Printing in Israel by Art Plus – Green Printing, Jerusalem

This book is dedicated to the memory of Jack, my devoted husband of sixty-four years, who encouraged and supported me throughout this journey; and to the memory of my dear cousin Cesia, with whom I shared my childhood; and to my children, Bill, Marc and Lois, Cheryl and Jay, Janet and Richard, and my grandchildren, Ilan, Alyssa and Andrew, Rebecca, Danny and Rachel, David, Jesse, Alex and Ben, in whom my memories live on.

CONTENTS

INTRODUCTION

T he story of Fanny Bienenfeld Lust and her nuclear family, all of whom survived the war, a rare occurrence during the Holocaust, spans three continents and many countries — Poland, Germany, Italy, Morocco, Spain, Portugal, and the United States of America.

The memoir begins with a happy and comfortable childhood in Maly Smykow, not far from the ancient city of Tarnów in southern Poland, on the estate of the family of Count Zborowski, the family's patron. With the escalation of antisemitism in Poland in the 1930s, the Bienenfelds relocated to Germany. However, during the Weimar Republic's final days and with the National Socialist Party's rise to power, the Jewish émigré family was at risk of being deported. Additionally, the patriarch became highly vulnerable, and the entire family faced great danger during Kristallnacht.

Since they were Polish citizens and had Polish passports, they returned to Poland believing that it would be safer for them than in Nazi Germany. Despite the surging antisemitism there, the Bienenfelds returned to Poland and settled in Kraków. After the Second World War began in September 1939, and Nazi Germany occupied Poland, the Jews fell prey to persecution, dispossession, and ghettoization.

During that period, once again, the confidence and determination of the matriarch saved the family. Undeterred by obstacles and hazards, she courageously managed to extricate her family from Poland to Italy, and then to northern Africa, Spain, and Portugal, until their final much-awaited journey to safety in the U.S.A. There, of all places, in the country that took them in and provided them with opportunities for rehabilitation and security, Fanny's brother was murdered in a hold-up — a disaster from which her parents never recovered.

In 1949, while in the U.S.A., Fanny again met her cousin Cesia, the last remaining scion of her extended family. She told Fanny in great detail about the fate of the Jews who were unable to escape from occupied Europe: they were murdered by the Nazis or interned in ghettos, concentration camps, or labor camps.

Cesia was one of the few Jews who managed to survive, due to the high-mindedness and kindness of a small minority, the Righteous Among the Nations, who had to keep their acts secret to avoid denunciation by their compatriots and to ensure the safety of their charges. After Cesia's escape from the Tarnów ghetto, the Myjkowskis, a Polish couple who risked their lives and made great sacrifices on her behalf, hid her in their home. They were among the few who cast rays of light into the abyss of antisemitism in Poland.

This book sheds light on the special personality of Regina Bienenfeld, the author's mother. As a teenager, her fortitude allowed her to survive and take action on behalf of her family under the threat of great risk. As a young woman, her self-confidence and determination, combined with her refusal to give up, served her well in choosing a husband and establishing a family. After the war began, as a maternal figure with strong views, she took the fate of her husband and children into her hands and led them to a safe haven.

Remembering Regina presents the Holocaust from a less familiar angle of the few Jews who managed to make their precarious way out of the continent, escaping from occupied Europe during the early years of the war. Regina stands out in this story, as told by her devoted daughter Fanny, as the mother who fought like a lioness to save her family.

— Bella Gutterman

PART ONE

MY MOTHER'S STORY

THE STORYTELLER

My mother was no ordinary woman. At ninety-five, she was as independent as she had been her entire life. When she could no longer do what she had always been able to do, she lost her will to live.

I tried to encourage her by telling her she had lived a full and rich life and succeeded in saving her family: "That was by far your greatest achievement — something you can really be proud of." "So where did it get me?" "If not for you, we would never have escaped from Hitler's clutches." "That's true," she answered reluctantly, "but I did not save my sister, and I will never forgive myself for that." "You would have had to delay leaving Poland and put your own family at risk," I reminded her, but she was not convinced.

It is impossible to give you a true picture of who my mother really was. She was larger than life. She knew who she was and stood up for what she believed in. However, there are sides of my mother I will never be able to understand.

My mother was a wonderful storyteller with an amazing talent for bringing her stories to life. These remain her greatest legacy to me. Only through them did I come to know what an extraordinary woman she was. Having heard them throughout my childhood, they became so familiar to me that I often thought I had actually been there myself. Fascinated, listening to her every word, I felt I had become her confidante. When she had finished telling me a story, I was immersed in her world, in a time and place not my own.

Although I was very young when my mother first started telling me her stories, I sensed that my role as her listener was to make her feel good, rather than to bring us closer together. I waited and hoped that we would connect somehow, but soon realized that my function was only to fulfill her needs. I was disappointed that she focused only on her own satisfaction and seeking my approval. But, ultimately, I was grateful to have had the opportunity to spend some rare moments with my mother, regardless of her intentions.

Regina Bienenfeld, Fanny's mother, 1939

Fanny and Regina, c. 1929

THE LETTER

My mother was born on December 18, 1898, in Galicia,[1] then a part of Poland ruled by the Austro-Hungarian Empire. Named Rivka at birth, and later known as Regina, she was the fourth child of Psachye and Feige Honig. Her father was an overseer on Count Zborowski's estate, an unusual occupation for an Orthodox Jew, a position given to him after an event that took place several years earlier.

During the 1890s' unrest in the Polish districts, Wolf Fallek, Psachye's future father-in-law, and his wife, Sarah, saved Count Menczinski, Zborowski's father-in-law, by hiding him in their cellar for six weeks. Count Zborowski never forgot this and was forever grateful to Wolf's family. After Wolf's daughter, Esther, married Psachye, the Count leased Maly Smykow,[2] part of his large estate, to them at very good terms. The young couple moved into a farmhouse with a courtyard in the front. The view from there, overlooking orchards and green pastures, crossed by a stream, was beautiful. Esther and Psachye often had their meals in the courtyard under the shade of the giant oak trees.

My grandfather, Psachye, a religious but progressive man, was a Talmud scholar, and, in addition to Hebrew and Yiddish, was fluent in both Polish and German. I remember my mother telling me that he was often called upon to arbitrate disputes between Jews and non-Jews.

My grandmother, Feige, was Psachye's second wife. His first wife, Esther, Feige's sister, died giving birth to their third child, leaving my grandfather with three small children: Jacob, Norbert, and a newborn baby girl called Hencia.

After Esther got married and started a family in Poland, Feige immigrated to the U.S.A., where she went to live with her sister, Welke, who was married and lived in New York's Lower East Side.

---

1   Galicia is a region in southeastern Poland and northwestern Ukraine. Until 1772, it was in Poland, and then became part of the Austro-Hungarian Empire. After the First World War, it was partitioned between Poland and Austria. Galicia was a great Jewish center teeming with religious and cultural life, including the developing *Haskala* (Jewish Enlightenment) movement.

2   "Little Smykow" – predominantly an agricultural area, dotted with small villages and farms.

My grandmother loved her adopted country and her life seemed to be going well until the day she received a letter from home. "Dear Feigele," her mother wrote in Yiddish, "Your sister, Esther, is very weak after giving birth to a baby girl. We need you to come home to help us with the children until she regains her strength."

Upset and somewhat puzzled by the news from home, Feige was not convinced that her sister's weakness was a sufficient reason to go back to Poland. But, what excuse could she give her mother for not returning? After all, she was not married, and did not have a family to keep her from leaving. Confused, Feige asked her sister what to do. Welke then told Feige in no uncertain terms that she must go back to help their sister Esther or she might live to regret it. Intimidated by her sister, Feige booked passage on the next ship leaving for Poland, but could not help feeling that she was making a mistake.

During the long journey, Feige had a strange dream. She woke up with a start, her heart pounding. For a moment, she did not know where she was, and then remembered she was on a ship taking her back to Poland. In the dream, Esther appeared and begged her to be a mother to her children. "Ich bet dech Feigele,"[3] she pleaded in Yiddish, "Sei eine Mame zu meine Kinder." The thought that Esther might be dead went through her mind. Then, she said to herself, "I'll see Esther as soon as I get home!"

Exhausted from the journey and upset by the dream, Feige arrived home. Her mother, Sarah, was waiting for her. After they embraced, Feige told her mother that she had to see Esther right away. "But you just got here," Sarah protested, "first, rest and get a good night's sleep." "You don't understand," Feige insisted, "I must see Esther to make sure she is all right." When Sarah saw how determined she was, she had no choice but to tell her the truth. Sarah paused for a few seconds to collect herself and took on a softer tone. "Feige, I don't know how to tell you, but Esther is no longer in this world." Feige gasped, "What happened? When did she die?" "The baby was big and the midwife could not stop the bleeding," Sarah explained, as she started to cry. "We tried to help her, but Esther's strength gave out. There was nothing we could do."

Both of them fell silent. Still in shock, Feige thought about what she had just heard, "So Esther was already dead when Mother wrote that letter.

---

3   "Feigele, I beg of you to be a mother to my children."

She deliberately lied to me, and tricked me into coming home. I am the only unmarried sister in this family and now that I am back, I will have to marry my widowed brother-in-law!" Outraged at being forced to return home under false pretenses, Feige stood up and faced her mother. "Now I see why you did not tell me Esther was dead. You were afraid that if you told me, I would not come back. Do you realize what you have done? You have ruined my life. Psachye could have married someone else; it did not have to be me! I will never forgive you for this," Feige cried. Fearing that she would become violent if she were left alone with her mother for another minute, she stormed out of the room.

Alone in her room, Feige was overcome by a paralyzing hopelessness. She wrung her hands in desperation and felt trapped into having to marry a man she hardly knew. "My mother and my sister Welke schemed to make me come back. What am I going to do now?" she cried, pounding her pillow and sobbing inconsolably. Finally, Feige fell into a deep sleep that mercifully blotted out the reality that had changed her life forever.

Sarah, however, did not care how angry her daughter was. Her mission was accomplished, and that was all that mattered to her. "How could I stand by and let a stranger take care of my precious grandchildren? Feige is their aunt. She will be good to them. I know I did the right thing. Feige will come to realize that, she will get used to Psachye, and everything will be all right." But nothing was ever right again between Feige and her mother. Feige never forgave her.

The wedding took place a few days later. It was a small, ritual event. After the customary breaking of the glass, Feige and Psachye were declared man and wife. Their marriage, like many in those days, was one of convenience. Feige tried to do her best to adjust to her new life. She took care of Esther's three children, as her sister requested in the dream, and began accepting this as her fate.

LIFE IN MALY SMYKOW

In 1893, Feige gave birth to a son, Leo, and when he was two years old, she gave birth to a girl, whom she named Esther, after her sister, but, sadly, the baby became ill and died. Feige was heartbroken over the loss of her daughter. She fell into a deep depression, but, during that time, my grandmother became pregnant with my mother. As I listened to my mother's childhood memories, I understood that she had never been nurtured. My grandmother, in her depression, was afraid to form an attachment to my mother for fear of losing her too, so she withdrew from her newborn baby, and a wet nurse was hired.

It took several years for my grandmother to recover from her depression, and then the family continued to grow. She had five more children after my mother. The first was Helen, followed by another girl, Clara. A year later, Hella, the sister to whom my mother was closest, was born. Paul, the only other boy besides Leo, came next. And lastly, another baby girl, Frieda, was born. Together with Esther's three children, the Honig family now had twelve members.

After having children of her own, my grandmother felt compelled to take care of them all, even though she never had a chance to live a life of her own choosing. My mother often heard her say, "Someday when my children are grown up I will go back to the U.S.A." I can only imagine the sadness my mother must have felt knowing that her mother was wishing away their time together.

While my grandmother was busy taking care of her large family, she had to leave the discipline to her husband. She did not always approve of his methods, but never interfered. My mother told me that her father would not tolerate any disturbance during dinner, and found an effective way to have peace and quiet. If one of the children misbehaved, he would smack the child sitting closest to him. As a result, none of his children wanted to sit next to him, so that was the last seat taken at the dinner table. After a few displays of such disciplinary action, everyone behaved.

A great deal of cooking had to be done every day, but especially on Fridays, when my grandmother had to get up earlier than usual to do all her work before the Sabbath began. She baked on Thursdays to allow enough time for the *challah*[4] dough to rise. The house smelled delightful and everyone looked forward to the Sabbath meals.

Before the meal started, my grandfather made the blessing over the wine. Then, everyone washed their hands. No one was allowed to talk until after the blessing for the *challah*, after which my grandfather would cut it into pieces and pass them around the table. Then, dinner was served, usually starting with fish, followed by soup with finely cut noodles made by my grandmother, and then roasted chicken, potatoes, and, of course, carrots, symbolizing fertility. *Meren*, the Yiddish word for a carrot dish, also means to multiply, and hence the carrot's special place in the family meal.

My mother remembered Passover as the busiest time of the year. All the inside walls in the house were whitewashed to make them fresh and clean. The dishes, pots, and pans used during the year had to be put away, and all household items kept for Passover use only were taken out of storage. Any leftover food not kosher for Passover was removed from the house, and either sold or given away. The *matzot* were baked under strict supervision by a *kashrut*[5] inspector. More fowl than usual was ritually slaughtered because the holiday lasted for eight days. Goose or chicken fat, *schmaltz*, was used in the cooking. The fat was stored in jars and used for Passover as well as during the year. My mother always looked forward to eating *grieven*, fried goose-skin pieces.

Every Passover, new outfits were bought for all the children. All these preparations were a great deal of work for my grandmother, but when everyone was finally seated at the table, dressed in their finery, she looked on with pride at her beautiful family. My grandfather sat at the head of the table, dressed in a *kittel*,[6] with Feige next to him. He enjoyed this role as the patriarch the most. He sat leaning to the left on a pillow, symbolizing freedom, preparing to retell the exodus of the Jews from Egypt. Before the *seder*[7], the *afikoman*[8] was carefully hidden by my grandfather. After the youngest boy

---

4   Special Sabbath bread.

5   Jewish dietary law.

6   A white robe worn by Jewish men on special occasions to signify purity, holiness, new beginnings, as well as a burial shroud.

7   The special service and meal on the first night/s of Passover.

8   A piece of *matzo* set aside to be eaten after the *seder* meal.

recited *Ma Nishtana*[9] the children would scramble from their seats to look for the *afikoman*, and the lucky one who found it would get whatever he or she asked for.

"There were many special dishes that we ate only during Passover," my mother told me. "One was *matzo* ball soup, served only on *seder* nights, which was everyone's favorite." As customary, at the end of the *seder*, one of the children had to open the door to let Elijah the Prophet in to "drink" a special cup of wine that was set aside for him. "When it was my turn," my mother said, "I was always afraid that Elijah would really walk in! While we were all watching to see if Elijah was coming, my father quickly emptied the cup of wine set aside for him, and told us that the Prophet's ghost had drunk it."

"When Passover was finally over, as wonderful as it was, we could not wait to have some bread and butter and get back to our normal routine."

MOVING TO ZGLOBICE

As the children got older, my grandparents realized they should move closer to a larger city so that their children could attend a public school and get a good secular education. Count Zborowski owned another estate in Zglobice,[10] which was only six kilometers from the thriving city of Tarnów.[11] There was a large Jewish community there, and their children would be able to attend the public schools while boarding with a Jewish family in the town. Psachye asked Count Zborowski if he could relocate him and his family to Zglobice. The Count, who was very fond of Psachye, agreed to lease part of his estate to him, situated on a hill overlooking the Dunajec River on the

9   A song, The Four Questions, chanted or sung during the *seder*.

10   Zglobice is a village in the Tarnów district in southern Poland, a few kilometers northwest of the city of Tarnów and east of Kraków. Established in the fourteenth century, on the western bank of the Dunajec River, it was owned by the Zbylitowski family. Another aristocratic family, the Moszczynieckis, whose name was corrupted to Menczinski, lived there. In the nineteenth century, the village and the estate became the property of Count Zborowski's family.

11   Tarnów is one of the oldest cities in Poland. Jews first settled there in the fifteenth century and were well integrated into the local economic system. On the eve of the Second World War, some 25,000 Jews lived there, accounting for 55 percent of the municipal population.

main road leading to Tarnów. The farmhouse, surrounded by orchards and an abundance of various fruit trees nearby, was large enough to accommodate their family.

My mother told me about the plums she would eat while they were still green: "They usually gave me a stomachache, but I did not care because I liked their sour taste. At the back of the house, there was a large vegetable garden, where we… would pick what we wanted to cook for dinner. There was also a magnificent flower garden on our estate, and I would often see the gardener cutting flowers for the mansion. The only thing I didn't like about moving to Zglobice was boarding out during the week. I would have preferred to stay at home and just get up earlier to travel to school. But such an arrangement was not possible, so I had to remain in Tarnów during the week. All week long, I would look forward to coming home for the weekend." My mother did not mind being in Tarnów during the winter months, but when it started getting warmer, she longed to be back in Zglobice, to enjoy her carefree days of summer outdoors.

More than anything, she missed her mother and constantly worried about her health: "My mother was always so tired, and even with the help, she was terribly overworked. The only time I saw her sit down was when she was mending our clothes. I would often sit by her to keep her company, and she would tell me wondrous tales about the U.S.A. Sometimes she even sang some of the nursery rhymes she learned from the children when she worked there as a nanny. I cherished those few precious times with my mother… when we were alone together, and she was mending clothes or braiding my hair."

The Count's wife, Alexandra, befriended my grandmother, whom she would often ask to accompany her on visits to sick and poor farmers who lived near the estate. They would bring them baskets of food and medicine and explain to the women how to take care of their sick. Always very busy with her husband and children, my grandmother welcomed those opportunities to spend some time away from the demands of her growing family, in another woman's company. Because of this friendship, my mother was often invited to play with the Countess's children, Alex and Irene. The Count and his family lived in a mansion within walking distance from the farmhouse, and my mother always looked forward to visiting his children. On those occasions, my grandmother dressed my mother in her finest clothes, and, while braiding her hair, reminded her to be on her best behavior.

She was dropped off by one of their own servants and had to ring a large pull-bell at the front door. A butler dressed in tails and white gloves would open the door, bowing slightly, as he let her in, and she would then follow him down the long hallway. Both sides of the walls were covered with portraits of the family ancestors, which my mother found frightening.

"The eyes on the portraits seemed to be following me," my mother explained, "and I had to turn my head away to avoid looking at them. I breathed a sigh of relief when I got to the playroom where Alex and Irene were waiting for me. They welcomed me with a big 'Hurray!' Their governess, a proper looking young woman, spoke only French to the children. While we played together, she would sit on a nearby bench reading her book, but always kept a watchful eye on us. I would follow Alex and Irene through the gate into the garden, where I was immediately transported into another world. I was glad that they ran ahead of me; I was in no hurry, wanting to feast my eyes on the splendor there. I was almost overcome by the sweet honeysuckle fragrance. Bees darted from flower to flower, stopping only to draw in nectar, and then disappeared from sight. Although I heard Irene calling, 'Rivka, where are you?' I did not answer; I wanted to linger just a little longer. Suddenly, Irene was standing in front of me. 'There you are,' she said, breaking the spell of the magical moment." Looking at my mother, I saw that her eyes were glazed. Once again, she had drifted into the past, and briefly seen herself as a child again.

During those storytelling sessions, I really got to know my mother. At such times, we shared a certain intimacy we did not have in our day-to-day lives. My mother was always so busy helping my father in the business that there was little time left for us to be together. I looked forward to those special times, but never knew when they would come.

MY GRANDMOTHER'S DEATH

My mother, a strong and confident woman, rarely showed any sign of vulnerability. The only time she let her guard down — besides after our great tragedy later in life — was when she spoke about the events around her mother's death.

She always started telling the story with these words: "I was only nine years old when my mother died, in 1907." Tears would well up in her eyes and she had to stop talking to compose herself. "We were already seven children; five girls and two boys. Frieda, the baby, was six months old when my mother realized she was pregnant again. She did not want another child and decided to have an abortion. My mother could not tell my father since she knew that he would never allow it. She could not confide in her mother because their relationship had suffered as a result of the deception about Esther's death. There was no one to turn to, and anxious to get it over with, Feige found someone to carry out the procedure. I can imagine how badly my mother must have felt with no one to dissuade or comfort her." My mother said, starting to cry, "All I know," she continued, wiping her eyes, "is that after the abortion, my mother began to hemorrhage and no one could stop the bleeding. The doctor somehow managed to have my mother admitted into a hospital, but she continued to lose blood. As weak as my mother was, she sensed that she was not going to recover. She asked that Leo, then fourteen, and I come to the hospital to see her.

"When my brother and I walked into her room we could not believe that this pale and weak-looking woman was our mother. She was asleep, but woke up a few minutes later. A wan smile appeared on her lips when she saw us at her bedside. She motioned to us to come closer, and when we did, she took Leo's hand into hers. She briefly closed her eyes, then looked at my brother and said, 'Leo, my son, I want you to promise me something.' Leo nodded his head, trying hard not to cry. 'I want you to promise me that you will always be like a father to your sisters and brother. It might seem an unusual request, but I know your father will surely marry soon after I am gone.' Leo let out a deep sob that tore at my heart, but my mother continued. 'Please promise me you will do as I have asked.' 'I promise,' Leo said, with tears rolling down his cheeks. I wanted to tell my mother to stop talking that way, but the words would not come out of my mouth. 'So that you will be able to carry out my wish,' my mother continued, 'I place my children's fate in your hands, my son.' With that commitment, my mother signaled to me to come closer, too. She sat up with great effort and placed her hands on top of our heads. As she did this, she murmured a prayer, and blessed and kissed us. Relieved, she then lay back in her bed, closed her eyes and went to sleep." My mother wiped her eyes, waited a few seconds, and said, "That was the last time I saw my mother."

Then she continued, "The morning after our visit to the hospital, I went to school, hoping against hope that my mother would recover. As I walked into my classroom, listless and forlorn, I noticed that my classmates were standing in a huddle. As soon as they saw me, they scrambled to their seats, except for the carpenter's daughter. She approached me and whispered gravely, 'My father got an order early this morning to make a coffin for your mother.' For a moment, I stood with my eyes riveted to the floor. Then, after staring at the girl in disbelief, I quickly turned and fled. I must go home, I told myself, with my heart pounding. I have to find out whether it is true. Oh God, please, please, make it not be true, I begged. I ran and ran. My mother can't be dead. That stupid girl must have been lying. I saw her only yesterday, I reasoned in desperation, trying to cling to some hope. I do not know how my legs carried me over the six kilometers to Zglobice, but when I finally made it home, I stood breathlessly at the door, then flung it open. When I saw my father's face, I knew that my mother was dead. My legs gave way and I sank to the floor."

"Throughout the week of *shiva*,[12] strange men I had never seen before came twice a day to say *kaddish*.[13] Knowing how much Leo loved our mother, I could not understand how he was able to say this memorial prayer, day after day, without breaking down. Our household was in a state of confusion, with the older children helping the younger ones. Hencia, then about 15, took care of the youngest ones, Paul and Frieda, who constantly cried for Mother. Friends of the family brought us food, but I could not eat anything. My throat hurt and my eyes were swollen. Wherever I went, I saw my mother. The chair she used to sit on while mending, or braiding my hair, now stood empty. I wandered around the house like a lost soul, isolating myself from my family. The pain in my heart did not go away and I can still feel it whenever I think of her."

12 *Shiva*, meaning seven, is the seven-day mourning period in Jewish tradition.
13 The Jewish memorial prayer for the dead.

MY GRANDFATHER REMARRIES AGAIN

As my grandmother predicted, my grandfather married shortly after the minimum thirty-day mourning period. "I was angry with my father," my mother told me. "I felt that he had betrayed my mother. Gittel, the woman my father married, a widow and his distant cousin, had a daughter from a previous marriage. My stepsister was also called Rivka, and because she was younger and a little shorter than me, we called her Kleine (Little) Rivka. I liked her, and, had my father not married her mother, we probably would have been good friends."

Fanny's grandfather and step-grandmother, Psachya and Gittel

"As one of the oldest girls in the family, I was expected to help with the youngest children, Paul and Frieda. Paul was almost three years old and still not toilet-trained. My stepmother constantly reminded me to change his diapers. 'He's your brother,' she would say. But I was rebellious and uncooperative, and refused to help with the chores. Kleine Rivka was a good soul and often did my chores for me. Although I appreciated her help, I never thanked her for it. I viewed both my stepsister and her mother as intruders, and resented the latter because she took my mother's place."

"One day, as I passed the kitchen, I overheard my stepmother criticizing my late mother for having been a poor housekeeper. My feelings of anger, which I had tried to suppress, suddenly exploded. Enraged, I hit my unsuspecting stepmother repeatedly. 'How dare you find fault with my mother's housekeeping!' I screamed. 'Don't ever let me hear you say anything about her again.' Then I stormed out of the room, slamming the door behind me. At first, I felt good for defending my mother, but later regretted my violent reaction. I dreaded facing my father and was afraid of what he might do. Later that day, I overheard my stepmother telling my father what I had done. He listened, but said nothing. I was surprised by his reaction, but I remembered a sentence he often quoted from *Pirke Avot*,[14] and understood why I was not punished: "Be deliberate in judgment." There was no doubt in my mind that my father did not condone my behavior toward his new wife, but I suspect that he felt I had suffered enough losing my mother and didn't want to add to my grief."

The years after her mother's death were the most difficult for my mother. She could not accept her stepmother, and their relationship went from bad to worse. Gittel was angry because my mother was never punished for hitting her. Frustrated by her rebellious attitude, she retaliated by verbally abusing my mother. "I'm sure Gittel was often tempted to raise her hand to me," my mother told me, "but probably controlled herself, remembering the time I hit her in my mother's defense. So, she told me over and over again how ugly I was, and how I would probably end up being an old maid. 'What man would want to marry a skinny girl like you?' she would say. After a while, I started believing her and became more depressed than I already was. The possibility that my stepmother's prediction might come true and I'd be stuck living with her for the rest of my life, scared me the most."

14   Ethics of the Fathers, Chapter 1, 1.

"All you had to do," I would say to my mother, "was to look in the mirror and see for yourself that you were far from ugly." Actually, my mother was quite attractive. She had high cheekbones and a turned-up nose that was the envy of many. Her blue-green eyes changed color according to the shade of clothes she was wearing. I suspect that Gittel was jealous of my mother's good looks since she was not an attractive woman herself.

ESCAPING TO CZECHOSLOVAKIA

A year after the First World War began, the Russian army attacked Galicia, where my mother's family was living. Fearing for the safety of his family, my grandfather took his wife and their children, except for Clara, and fled south, by horse and wagon, to Czechoslovakia. They traveled for many days along rough roads until they finally reached Muttersdorf.[15] My grandfather immediately sought the assistance of the local Jewish community to help him find accommodation for his exhausted family. Despite all the efforts on their behalf, they went through a terrible time of hardship and suffering. Whether it was the poor food while traveling, or lack of proper sanitation, all the children became very ill. Although treated by local doctors, they did not respond well and had to be hospitalized. After many weeks of fighting their illnesses, the children recovered and were sent home. My mother made only one brief reference to that terrible time in her life. In Muttersdorf, as a result of contracting typhoid fever, she lost her beautiful, thick hair that her mother had always enjoyed braiding. Eventually, her hair grew back, but not as thick as before.

While my mother's family was in Czechoslovakia, the Austrian army, together with their German allies, counter-attacked, forcing the Russians to retreat to the East. In the fury at their defeat, the Russians launched their scorched-earth policy, setting fire to farms and estates along their path. They plundered whatever they could, including the cattle and horses they rounded up. The Ukrainians among the retreating Russians instigated antisemitic pogroms, lashing out at large number of Jews living among them. The native Polish population joined in these pogroms, in which 100,000 Jews were

---

15   Muttersdorf is an ancient city in Bohemia.

brutally murdered. My mother's grandfather, Wolf, who was trampled to death by the retreating Cossacks, was among the victims. My mother's sister, Clara, who was living with her grandparents at the time, witnessed the horror of her grandfather's death.

MY MOTHER'S RETURN TO ZGLOBICE

After the Armistice of Compiègne agreement was signed, Marshal Piłsudski defeated the Russians, and proclaimed Poland's independence.[16] His reputation as a tolerant leader spread, and many Jews who had fled from Poland felt it was safe to return home.

My grandfather, after living in exile for almost two years, wanted to return to Poland with his family, but they had exhausted almost all their funds while living in Czechoslovakia. He did not know how he would feed his family without an income. Out of sheer desperation, he took my mother aside and told her about his problem. She was shocked to hear this news and asked her father what they were going to do. "The only thing we can do," my grandfather told her, "is to reopen the *karczma* (pub) we ran before the war. I would ask Norbert or Leo to help me, but there is no telling when they will be coming back from the army. You are the only one who can help me. Would you consider going back home by yourself to open our *karczma*? Then, when we all return home we would at least have some money."

"I was totally taken aback by my father's request," my mother told me, "but also flattered by his confidence in me. He looked so distraught that I just did not have the heart to refuse him." 'It would be a good time to open the *karczma*,' my grandfather told her. 'Soldiers are returning from the war and will be pleased to have a place where they can have a drink and get something to eat.' My grandfather then explained to her what she would have to do if she went back home. He then said, 'I know you can do anything you set your mind to.' Seeing how relieved he was, I agreed to go. Then he added, 'I think it would be best if you leave in the morning.' My father was right. There was no

16   On November 11, 1918, after surrendering, Germany signed an armistice agreement in a railroad car in France. Subsequently, this would be considered an affront to Germany's national honor.

point in putting off the trip. I quickly went to pack my bag, and then got ready for bed. I lay awake for a long time thinking about what lay ahead of me."

"Early the next morning, after I said goodbye to my sisters and brother, my father took me to the train station. He looked worried, but I pretended not to notice. When the train pulled in, he hugged me again. 'Be careful,' he said, with tears in his eyes. I handed my bag to the conductor and climbed aboard quickly, stood by the window, and waved to my father. As the train chugged out of the station, I continued waving until my father's figure disappeared into the distance, and wondered when I would see him again."

"The dreary landscape, dotted with cattle, rushed past my window, and I soon fell asleep. After a long, monotonous trip, I arrived in Tarnów, and hired a *droshka*[17] to take me to Zglobice, which was about six kilometers away. I knew the road well since I had gone by that route on the day I found out that my mother had died."

"Soon we approached an area that looked familiar. I strained to see our house, barely noticing the destruction the Russians had left behind. What if our house was destroyed like some of the homes I had seen along the way? What would I do? I worried, and then started panicking. My father had not prepared me for this. All at once, I caught sight of our house standing forlorn in the gloom of the setting sun. I breathed a deep sigh of relief and told the driver to stop the carriage. The driver brought the carriage to a stop and carried my bag to the door. I paid him absentmindedly, and waited until the sound of the horse's hooves faded away. A strange silence enveloped me as I slowly walked toward the house. My heart was pounding. The lock on the door was broken, and I made a mental note to have it fixed. The door creaked painfully as I slowly pushed it open."

"Inside, the house looked familiar, but not quite the way I had remembered it. The emptiness drained the house of the life it had once had. I looked around, not sure what for, and then saw our dining room table standing proudly in the middle of the empty room, as if it had defied destruction by the enemy. I walked over to it and gently stroked its dusty surface. 'I'm glad you made it through,' I said to myself as I remembered the times we had all sat around it covered with a white cloth, waiting for the Sabbath meals to begin." Overcome by emotion, my mother suddenly stopped. I suggested she take a

17   A driver of a horse and carriage.

break. She nodded, unable to speak. After she regained her composure, she continued her story.

"Suddenly, an overwhelming feeling of relief swept over me, and I heard myself say, 'We have our house. Thank God, our house was spared.' Exhausted, I relaxed and finally fell into a deep sleep. After a good night's sleep, and relieved of my anxieties, I walked over to tell our neighbors I was back. When they opened the door, they looked at me as if I were a ghost returned from the dead. I explained that I had come back from Czechoslovakia, where we had been during the war, and was going to reopen our *karczma*. I asked them if they would help me get it ready for business. Still in shock, they readily agreed, we shook hands, and I promised them the first drinks on the house. I could not help laughing. When I looked back, I saw them shaking their heads in disbelief as they walked back into the house."

"Our *karczma*, which was in a separate wing adjoining the house, had miraculously escaped serious damage. Apparently, the retreating Russians had discovered an abundance of liquor and drank to their heart's content before they left without doing any mischief. I checked whether I had enough glasses, and was glad I would not have to buy any. The tables and chairs were upturned, and the place really needed a good cleanup. I got the food and liquor supplies on the black market, as my father had suggested, and realized I would be able to open up much sooner than expected. Word soon got around that a *karczma* was open, and local farmers and returning soldiers started patronizing the place. At first, I found it hard to manage by myself, but soon I got used to it."

"When the son of Jewish neighbors heard that I was operating the *karczma* alone, he offered to come over and help me open and close up the place every morning and evening. I gratefully accepted his offer and was glad to have someone I knew and could trust to look out for me."

To prevent her customers from getting drunk, my mother cleverly limited the drinks to two per person, and, if people complained about it, she blamed it on the shortage.

A few days after she had opened the *karczma* for business, my mother noticed a young Russian officer sitting across from where she was working. He had been coming for several days and was watching her. That particular day, he stayed longer than usual. After business had slowed down, he walked over to the bar and introduced himself. He told my mother he was a medical doctor and was returning to Moscow in a few days after serving at the front for a year. "I hope I am not being presumptuous," he started to say, "but my curiosity got the better of me. I have been watching you for several days now and noticed that you are working here all by yourself, and if that is true, may I ask why?" "I was surprised to be questioned by a stranger," my mother told me, "and didn't really want to engage in any conversation, but was impressed by the officer's polite manner. I didn't want to be rude and felt there was no harm in telling him why I was working by myself. 'You see,' I told him, 'after the war started, my family fled to Czechoslovakia, and stayed there for over a year and a half. The funds we were living on had run dangerously low. Without an income to fall back on, my father asked me to return to Poland and reopen our *karczma*. Since my two brothers are serving in the army, I was the only one he could count on to help him.' The officer replied, 'You mean to tell me that your father sent you, a girl in her late teens, all by herself, to open up a *karczma*? Wasn't he afraid that you could run into harm's way? Why, any one of these men here could get drunk and molest you!' The officer seemed outraged."

"'I am not afraid,' my mother answered calmly. 'I limit the drinks to two per person so there is not much chance of them getting drunk. I am also very fortunate to have a good neighbor who comes twice a day to help me. So you see there is no reason for concern.' But the officer persisted, 'If you had an opportunity to get out of this predicament, would you consider leaving? I would be happy to take you back to Russia with me. My mother would take good care of you until my discharge and then we could get married.' 'Thank you for the offer,' my mother said, trying not to show how surprised she was by his sudden proposal. 'I am not in any predicament. I am only fulfilling an obligation to my family. Do you think I could just get up and leave when they are depending on me?' I said a little angrily."

The officer had not expected the answer my mother gave him, but was impressed by her loyalty to her family. "I would have considered myself very lucky had you accepted my offer, but I understand that your family must be very important to you. Women like you are hard to find these days," he said respectfully. "I envy the man you will marry someday." Stretching out his hand, he added, "I hope you have no hard feelings. I wish you luck and the safe return of your family." "He then picked up his hat, and looking back at me once again, he left."

After hearing that story, I wondered if that was all that had happened. Perhaps because of her traditional upbringing, my mother was reluctant to admit to a romance with this Russian officer.

"A few months later, as I was about to close up the *karczma*," my mother continued, "I saw a wagon approaching and heard familiar voices shouting, 'Rivka, where are you? We have come home!' I can't tell you how happy I was to see them all safe and sound," my mother continued. "I had not heard from them for a long time and was very worried. To tell you the truth," she confessed, "I was not sure how much longer I could have held out, working by myself day after day. At least I would get some relief now that my family was back. After the excitement of being back home died down, everyone went inside. I was glad that they had brought back some food supplies with them, probably because they heard about the terrible shortages in Poland. I found myself alone with my father and saw that he was in a state of shock. It must have hit him hard to see the devastation wrought by the Russians. 'We heard what the Russians had done to our country,' he said, 'but in my wildest dreams, I could not have imagined what I would see. I drove by Count Zborowski's estate — it was in shambles. I heard that the Count and his family had fled to France when we left. I am glad that they got out in time, or the Cossacks would have killed them all. What are we going to do?' he said, wringing his hands as he walked back and forth. 'Well, at least we have the house,' I reminded him, 'and a roof over our heads.' 'Of course, I am glad we have the house, but I still have to put food on the table. We have very little money left, and the income from the *karczma* is not enough to feed us.'"

"'I forgot to tell you I heard from Leo just before we left.' My father told me that both Leo and Norbert had been discharged and were now living in Vienna. Leo said they planned to come home, but after they heard that Marshall Piłsudski was mobilizing all men of military age to help liberate Poland from the Russian occupation, they fled to Austria. Leo also mentioned that the firm he had worked for in Tarnów had relocated to Vienna, and had asked Leo to come and work for them. 'As much as I need them to help me,' my father told me, 'I can't take the chance of having them come home, only to be drafted again. I am going to write and tell them that the best way they can help is to send us money.'"

After Leo received my grandfather's letter, and heard in what dire straits the family was in, he immediately wired them a large sum of money.

He suggested that his father buy some livestock and start a milk round, which he thought was the best solution for the time being. When he received the money, my grandfather followed Leo's advice and bought several cows, but refused to go on the milk round. As my mother explained, her father was a proud man, and could not accept the fact that the war had brought him down from an estate manager to a penniless man. He told my mother that since she was the only one with some business experience, she would have to do it. My mother, by then a young woman of twenty, was embarrassed to do it. She told her father that providing for the family was not her responsibility. She reminded him that she had risked her life by coming back by herself to reopen the *karczma*, and stormed out of the room.

Her sister Clara, who had recently returned home from her stay with her grandparents after her grandfather was killed by the Cossacks, was relieved to be back. She tried to convince my mother to reconsider and take on the new responsibility. "You know Father is not going to relent on his decision," she said, "Imagine what Leo would say when he hears about this. He is certainly not going to tell Father that he has to do it." My mother agreed. There was no point arguing about it. If Leo found out that she had refused to take on the round, he would be very annoyed with her. "I know you have done more than your share to help us, but we have no choice," Clara said. She was right. Together with Clara, she went on the milk round, but vowed to never forgive her father for forcing her to do so.

MY MOTHER MEETS HER FUTURE HUSBAND

Anxious to move on with her life, my mother made an appointment with a matchmaker to discuss the kind of qualities she was looking for in a spouse. She emphasized that the proposed young man should come from a good family, be presentable, and be a good provider. Within a few weeks, the matchmaker came to see my mother and told her that she had found a suitable young man who met the necessary requirements.

The matchmaker said that he was of average height with brown eyes and dark hair. "His name is Eliezer and he lives in Dombrova. He currently works in his father's business and is a good businessman. He is about twenty-seven years old, the second child of four siblings … and is also quite handsome."

My mother expressed interest in meeting him and asked the matchmaker to arrange a date.

The night before her date with her future husband, my mother had an unusual dream. Her grandfather, Wolf, of whom she had always been very fond, appeared to her, and pointing to a young man seated at a table, said in Yiddish, "Dus werd dein chusen sein."[18] My mother did not think her dream was significant until she walked into the restaurant where the meeting was to take place. From a distance, she saw that the man at the table with their matchmaker looked exactly like the one her grandfather had pointed to in the dream.

The matchmaker spotted my mother coming in and noticed that she looked pale and a bit out of sorts. She asked my mother to sit down and quickly went to bring her a glass of water. Within a few minutes, my mother felt better and said she was ready to meet the young man. "The moment I saw him," my mother said, "I knew I was destined to marry him."

After they met a few times, they liked each other enough to get formally engaged. According to tradition, the future bride and groom, witnessed by a rabbi and members of both families, signed a written agreement. Afterward, the bride and groom were wished a hearty *Mazel Tov*, and schnapps and sponge cake were served.

My mother's brother, Leo, who was living in Vienna, was the first person to be informed of my mother's upcoming marriage. Although he was pleased to hear the good news, he wanted to look into the groom's background himself. He made additional inquiries and found that the young man had a pleasant disposition and came from a good family.

Leo gave his approval, and invited his sister to come to Vienna. He never forgot the words his dying mother said to him: "Always be a father to your sisters and brother." Leo wanted to fulfill his promise as best as he could. He told my mother that the visit's main purpose was to buy her a trousseau. He was a wealthy man at the time and could well afford to be generous to her.

My mother was very excited to be going to Vienna. She had never been in a big city before, but more than anything else, she looked forward to seeing her brother again. When she arrived, Leo was at the railroad station waiting for her. After giving her a warm welcome, Leo was anxious to hear the news from home. He inquired about each and every one of his siblings. On the way

18   He will be your future bridegroom.

to the hotel where my mother would be staying, Leo explained that he had engaged a professional shopper to accompany her on the many trips she would make to buy her trousseau. In addition to a new wardrobe, he was treating her to a new bedroom suite and other household items.

While my mother was busy shopping in Vienna, her future husband rented an apartment for them in the center of Tarnów on one of the main streets called Walowa.

The wedding was a simple, traditional affair. Regretfully, photographs were not taken, so I have never had the pleasure of seeing my mother dressed as a bride.

Based on his experience working with his parents, my father started what he hoped would develop into his own wholesale clothing business. After settling in, they were ready to start a family. My mother looked forward to being the kind of mother she had never had. Shortly after the wedding, she became pregnant, and, in time, gave birth to a beautiful blonde, blue-eyed boy, whom they named William, after my mother's grandfather, Wolf.

The birth of their firstborn would have been a great celebration had the baby not been born with clubfoot. My parents were beside themselves with grief and did not know what to do. My mother immediately got in touch with her brother. She had always trusted his judgment and knew that he would be able to give them good advice.

When Leo heard the terrible news, he assured my parents that clubfoot could be surgically corrected. He told them not to worry: he would find out which surgeon in Vienna was the best and most experienced in that field. Dr. Spitzer, a well-known orthopedic surgeon, agreed to operate on Willi, and told my parents to bring their baby to Vienna in six months. He would perform the operation, giving the baby enough time to heal so that by the time he turned one, he would be able to walk normally.

My parents were reassured, and trusted Leo's judgment in choosing the best surgeon. When Willi was six months old, my mother returned to Vienna with him for the operation. It had been only a year and a half since my mother had been in that beautiful city on a happier mission. Little did she know then that she would soon return with such a heavy heart.

My father stayed behind, hoping and praying that his son's operation would be successful. He could not concentrate on his business and was anxious to have this hurdle behind him. The operation was a huge success, and my parents felt as if a stone had been lifted off their hearts. Dr. Spitzer came out of the operating room with a big smile on his face. My mother recalled that he said, "I guarantee that your son will be walking in six months." "I kissed him with tears in my eyes, and told him we would never forget what he had done for us," she told me.

As Dr. Spitzer predicted, Willi was walking at exactly one year of age. I can imagine how thrilled my parents were when my brother took his first step. They could not believe the miracle that had taken place and thanked God over and over again for having answered their prayers.

Most of what I know about my mother's oldest brother, Leo, is from her stories. She always spoke about him with great respect, never forgetting that he had rescued her family from a life of poverty and hardship. But as loyal and devoted as her brother was, he was emotionally distant from his siblings and avoided getting involved in their lives. My uncle seemed to me rather distant and businesslike in his relationship with the family.

Whenever my mother came to his office for business advice, he would always greet her with, "What can I do for you?" instead of "How are you?" This impersonal greeting annoyed my mother so much so that she once answered, "You can give me a kiss!" She said it so spontaneously that it totally disarmed him. He smiled apologetically, realizing how rigid he sounded, but withheld the kiss just the same.

Thinking back on Leo's motivation to help his family in such an altruistic way, I wonder whether his mother's blessings to him on her deathbed motivated him. He may have believed that the blessings were not his alone and perhaps he felt they should have been shared with his siblings. My mother admired her brother throughout her life and she remained forever grateful to him until she died.

MY BIRTH

A year and a half after Willi's operation, in 1924, my mother was expecting again. Traumatized by her experience with my brother, she was very apprehensive. She was plagued by these thoughts: "What if it happens again, and this time it is a girl born with clubfoot? I don't think I could bear it. Perhaps, it would be better to abort the baby." I was surprised to hear my mother had even considered having an abortion, knowing that such a procedure had killed her own mother. Nevertheless, out of fear she went to see an abortionist, convinced it was the best thing to do. While waiting for her appointment at the doctor's office, she heard a woman scream out so loud that she lost her courage and ran out as fast as she could. That scream saved my life.

"After many hours of labor, I tried to sleep between pains. I remember calling out for my mother to help me. I felt cold compresses on my forehead, and thought my mother was there. 'Hold on, it won't be much longer,' I heard her say. It gave me courage, and just a few minutes later, you were born. Although exhausted, I first had to look at your feet to make sure they were all right. Then I could let myself fall asleep. Your father and I agreed to name you Feige, after my mother, but called you Fella. Later, when we moved to Germany, we changed your name to Fanny."

Fanny and Willi, age one and three respectively

Three months after I was born, my mother's brother, Norbert, and his wife, my Aunt Malla, had a baby girl. They named her Cesia, and, although we were different, we formed a special connection to each other. Cesia, a wiry child, did not like eating and gave her mother a hard time at mealtimes. She had very curly hair, which was very difficult to manage, high cheekbones, and slightly slanted eyes, making her look somewhat Asian. In contrast, I had straight brown hair cut in a bob, with bangs over my forehead. My eyes were dark brown like my father's and I had my mother's upturned nose.

Cesia looked up to me and always made me feel important. Our special attachment continued well into our teens.

PART TWO

MY STORY WITH MY MOTHER

AN EARLY MEMORY

I remember my mother more by her absence than by her presence.

I could not have been more than three years old; I woke up from my nap one day and found myself all alone in the bedroom I shared with my parents. The windows facing my crib were wide open and the see-through curtains were billowing into the room. Holding my doll, I sat mesmerized watching the curtains dance to the wind's rhythm. The house seemed unusually quiet and I did not hear any sounds from behind the bedroom door.

I kept on watching the curtains do their dance and wondered why no one was coming to see if I was awake. I finally heard footsteps coming towards the bedroom. I thought it would be my mother, but it was not her; it was a woman my mother had left me with while I was asleep. "Where is my mother?" I asked, disappointed to see this stranger. "I don't know," the woman answered, lifting me out of my crib, "but I am sure she will be back very soon." I wished the woman had left me in my crib to watch the curtains. By the time my mother returned it was too late to show her the dancing curtains, since the wind had died down and the curtains were hanging lifelessly.

MEMORIES OF MY FATHER

My father was a handsome man and always well groomed. He had dark brown eyes and a black beauty mark on the top of his right cheek of which he was very proud and which he liked people to notice. I cannot picture my father without a mustache, which he had for as long as I can remember. Sometimes I would watch him shave, and marveled at how long it took to trim his mustache. He had a special pair of scissors for that purpose, which I was warned never to touch.

Fanny's father, Lazer (Leo)

My father was a generous man and hardly ever refused to buy us anything we asked for, but he was also shy and could not express his affection for Willi and myself. Yet, he always remembered to bring us chocolate or other edible surprises when he came home. Early on, I realized his great admiration for my mother. He left the responsibility of raising us to her. However, they would always consult with each other on important business and family matters.

My parents rarely displayed their affection for each other in our presence. If Willi or I were within earshot when they were joking around, they would start speaking in Yiddish and whisper, "Not in front of the children."

Fanny's parents, Regina and Lazer (Leo)

I actually learned Yiddish from my father. Although he spoke German and Polish, he was most comfortable with Yiddish; had he not spoken to me in Yiddish, I would never have learned this most wonderful language.

My father's name was Eliezer, which was shortened to Lazer and then changed to Leo once we moved to Germany. He had three siblings: his brother, Yossel, was the oldest, then came my father, followed by his sister, Mindel, and his younger brother, Chaim. Unlike my mother, he hardly ever talked about his family, and so I know very little about them. Whenever I asked my father to tell me something about his mother, a sad look came into his eyes, and I would drop the subject. The only thing my father told me about my grandmother, Rachel, was that she had a heart condition and died when he was fifteen years old.

However, one story must have made a deep impression on him because my father told it to me many times. His parents had a wholesale clothing business in which they both worked together. One day, my grandmother did not come to work. It was an unusually busy day and my grandfather had a hard time taking care of all the customers. After he received a large sum of money, he was anxious to serve the next person. He hurriedly put the cash into a pair of boots and forgot to tell my grandmother about it. When she returned to work the next day, she sold the boots. I suspect that someone may have seen my grandfather put the money into the boots and came back the next day to see if he could buy them. Had my grandfather served the customer, he would have remembered that he had hidden the money there. There was a big to-do about this mistake, since a large amount of cash was lost. My father told me that it took a long time for his parents to recover financially after that.

* * *

My parents had been considering immigrating to Germany for a long time, and, after the stock market collapse in 1929, my father left Poland for Germany. It must have been a very difficult decision for him to make — to leave his wife and two children, not knowing what the future had in store for them.

While my father was away, my mother was busy making the arrangements for our departure from Poland. She was in and out of the house on errands. My brother, Willi, was already attending school so I was the only one who had to be looked after. I was often left in the care of Aunt Hella, my mother's younger sister, as I was that day. It had been only a few months after my father had left, and a huge box arrived from him, addressed to me. I was very surprised and could not imagine what my father had sent me. After my aunt opened the box and removed all the wrapping, I saw, lo and behold, that there was a magnificent doll's carriage with a life-size, real-looking baby doll inside, dressed in a blue knitted sweater and hat. I stood there with my mouth open. Aunt Hella, just as impressed as I was, said, "Your Papa must love you very much to have sent you such a wonderful present."

After I had recovered from my surprise, I asked my aunt if she could take me for a walk with my doll's carriage. We lived on the third floor and my aunt was not very keen to carry the doll's carriage down three flights of stairs, but I pleaded with her until she finally relented. "Before we go," she said, "you have to go to the bathroom." "But I don't have to go," I argued, eager to leave. "Are you sure?" Aunt Hella asked again. "I am sure," I said, nodding my head. I slipped on a sweater, held the door open for my aunt, and followed her down the stairs. We were on the ground floor when she handed me the dolls' carriage. I started walking proudly down the street, still unable to believe that the doll and carriage were actually mine. Heads were turning and passersby were remarking what a lucky girl I was. Halfway down the street, I felt that I was getting wet. Warm urine was slowly running down my legs into my shoes and socks. I kept on walking hoping Aunt Hella would not notice, but she was walking right behind me and saw what happened. She caught up with me, got hold of the carriage and led me into the hallway of a building, pulled down my panties and gave me a spanking, "I asked you if you had to go before we left," Aunt Hella scolded, "but you convinced me that you didn't. Now you have spoiled our day, and we have to go back home to change your clothes." My bottom was burning, but as much as it hurt, I did not make a sound. I knew Aunt Hella was right. I deserved that spanking and promised myself never to let that happen again.

LEFT WITH STRANGERS

One of my earliest recollections is of being left with strangers when I was only about four years old. Without telling me what she was about to do, my mother walked me to a ground floor apartment in the building where we lived. I wondered why, since we were not very familiar with those neighbors. After my mother knocked on the door, a woman opened the door only a crack and asked my mother what she wanted. My mother explained that she was a neighbor from the third floor. She told the woman that she had to go somewhere unexpectedly and asked her if I could stay with her, promising she would not be long. I do not remember what the woman said because when I heard that my mother was about to leave me with this strange woman, I burst into tears, begging her not to go. Ignoring my pleas, she began to walk away. I clung to her, but she freed herself from me and left.

The woman stood there bewildered and did not know what to do with this crying child left at her door. After she recovered from the surprise my mother sprung on her, she took me by the hand and walked me into her home. She tried to calm me down, reassuring me that my mother would be back soon, but the more she tried to console me, the harder I cried.

When her husband came home from work, he was surprised to find an unfamiliar child in the house. I was somewhat comforted, realizing his was a familiar face, having seen him come and go from their apartment several times. He asked his wife who I was and why I was there. Overhearing her telling her husband what had happened, I started crying all over again. He was a toy vendor, and carried his wares on his back. After hearing that my mother had left me with them, he came over to where I was sitting, bent down and spoke kindly to me: "If you promise to stop crying, I will let you pick out and keep any toy you like." I nodded, still sobbing, and pointed to a paper bird hanging on a stick. I had seen him holding those birds and whirling them around to show how they "flew" as he swung them from side to side. It was getting dark and my mother had not come back. About to have their dinner, the husband and his wife asked me if I wanted something to eat. I shook my head and said, "No, thank you." I had finally stopped crying and played with the bird until I fell asleep.

I do not know when my mother came back to pick me up, but the next morning when I woke up, I found the bird on my bed — the only reminder of the day my mother abandoned me. Many years later, I asked my mother why she had left me with strangers. She justified it by telling me I was too attached to her and she could never leave me with anyone. About two years later, in a similar incident, she left my brother and me with total strangers.

MY ZLOTY

A few weeks before we were to leave for Germany, in 1930, my paternal grandfather came with his daughter, Mindel, to say goodbye to us. It was the first time I remember meeting my paternal grandfather. I do not know why, but I was somewhat in awe of him. He had a gray beard and walked with a cane. He did not have a limp; perhaps he used the cane for effect. He said a brief hello to me, and since my mother was out on an errand, he decided to wait for her together with his daughter. They walked into the room next door to where the young woman looking after me at the time was helping me get dressed. I was sitting and while she was struggling to get my boots on over my shoes, I overheard my aunt and grandfather arguing. Before long, the argument grew more intense, and my grandfather stormed out of the room, telling his daughter he was not going to tolerate her shouting at him any longer. My aunt followed her father, and, as she went past, I said, "You know, Aunt Mindel, that is not a very nice way to talk to your father." My grandfather, who was already at the front door, overheard what I had said and turned back. He reached into his pocket and gave me a silver zloty,[19] and said, "Buy something you like," patted me on the head, and then left.

No one had ever given me so much money, and I carefully hid it. I knew exactly what I was going to buy with it, and did not tell anyone what my grandfather had given me. Across the street from where we lived was a fancy candy store. Every time I passed it, I would look in the window, and wish that I could buy my favorite candies, shaped like wild strawberries and sprinkled with sugar that made them sparkle. I think I liked how they looked more than their taste.

Willi was the only one I confided in about the zloty my grandfather had given me. My brother was very impressed. "That's a lot of money. What are you going to get?" he asked. "I want to get the strawberry candies I like, but

19   The Polish currency, which means a golden coin.

I am not allowed to cross the street, so would you please get them for me?" Willi, who was seven and a half years old, had permission to cross the street alone. "Okay," he said, "I'll get them for you." I gave him the zloty and he started crossing the street. The street was hilly, and my brother did not see the approaching car until it was too late. I heard the car screech to a halt and saw Willi on the ground. Stunned, I stood there watching helplessly. A crowd formed around the car. Then, I saw a man carry Willi to the side of the street where I was standing. Someone had recognized my brother and went to call my mother. Within a few minutes, my mother came running toward the man who was still holding Willi. "Is he all right?" she managed to ask, looking as white as a ghost. "Yes, I think he is okay," I heard him say. "The car stopped just in time." Willi came to, and my mother carried him up to our apartment.

"It's all my fault," I thought, as I followed my mother up the stairs. She asked Willi if he was sure that nothing was hurting him, and he shook his head. "I'll get a doctor to look at you, just to make sure," she said. She did not ask Willi why he had crossed the street, and he put his finger over his mouth, signaling to me not to tell. I walked silently behind them, feeling despondent. I heard my mother ask Willi again if he was all right. I wondered why she had not asked about me. She knew we had been together before the accident, but her concern was only for Willi, and not me. I expected her to turn around to see if I was behind them, but she never did.

LEAVING POLAND FOR BERLIN IN 1930

It was almost a year since my father had left Poland, which seemed so long ago that I barely remembered what he looked like. The doll's carriage he sent me from Germany was a constant reminder of how much he loved me. Willi and I sorely missed him and could not wait to see him again.

The apartment, now emptied of furniture, seemed strangely unfamiliar and we heard our voices echo in the empty rooms. A few days before we were going to leave, my mother was busy with some last-minute packing when the doorbell rang. It was the postman, delivering a letter for my mother. "Is the letter from Papa?" I asked excitedly. "No," my mother answered. "It's from Aunt Hella." My aunt and her family had moved to Germany in 1929. My mother tore open the envelope, anxious to read what her sister had written.

"What does Aunt Hella say?" I asked, noticing how upset my mother looked. "I'll tell you some other time," she answered. "But is she all right?" I insisted. "Stop pestering me," my mother answered impatiently, "yes, she's fine." My mother put the letter away and went back to packing our clothes. I knew something had upset her, but I did not ask any more questions.

On the day of our departure, I was surprised to see Uncle Norbert and Cesia waiting for us at the station. I was happy that they had come to see us off, but when Cesia and I were told it was time to say goodbye, we burst into tears and held on to each other, refusing to let go. Passersby looked at us curiously, wondering why we were so upset. My mother and uncle watched helplessly, unable to calm us down. When the conductor blew his whistle, signaling that it was time to board the train, we had to be separated, and my uncle picked Cesia up so that we could board the train. I watched teary-eyed from the window until my uncle and Cesia disappeared from sight. I was crying long after we left the station, not caring anymore about the train ride I had looked so forward to.

When we arrived in Berlin, my father was waiting for us. Welcoming us with open arms, he could not get over how much we had grown. A taxi was waiting, and we collected our baggage and left, anxious to see our new home.

A few days after our arrival, Willi and I became very ill. We both had a high fever and very sore throats. Worried, my parents called a doctor, who diagnosed diphtheria. I remember lying in my mother's bed, listless and unable to eat or drink. My throat hurt so much I could not even swallow water. My mother stayed at our bedsides and did everything she could to nurse us back to health.

I had barely recovered from my bout with diphtheria when I came down with whooping cough. Willi was immediately whisked away to Aunt Hella's for fear he would catch the dreadful disease. After many weeks, my cough finally subsided. To help clear my lungs, the doctor advised my mother to take me to Wannsee, a lake with a beachfront on the outskirts of Berlin, only a short train ride away from the city. It was mid-winter, and I was glad to spend the time alone with my mother. While we were on the train, I longed for my mother to put her arms around me and pull me close to her, but she was absorbed in her own thoughts, unaware of my presence.

On the beach, she sat watching me in silence, while I jumped from one ice patch to another at the edge of the water. Every now and then, she cautioned me to be careful, but then withdrew back into her thoughts. I had the feeling she would much rather be elsewhere than with me. She may have tried hard to be the mother she had wanted as a child, but could not be the mother I wished for.

After I recovered from whooping cough, I got the new doll I had wanted for a long time. She looked like a real baby and had a porcelain head with eyes that opened and closed. She soon became my favorite doll and I would play with her for hours on the enclosed balcony in our apartment. While I was undressing the doll one day, she slipped out of my hands and fell on the terrazzo floor. Her head shattered into many pieces and I stood horrified, staring at my beloved doll. Broken hearted, I picked her up and ran to my mother. "Look what happened," I cried, tears streaming down my face. "Please, Mutti," I begged, "buy me another doll like that." "You have enough dolls to play with," she said. "But she is my favorite doll," I pleaded, trying to convince her how much the doll meant to me. "I am not buying you another doll," my mother said, not acknowledging how upset I was. "Now leave me alone," she said, "and don't talk to me about it anymore."

Heartsick at my mother's indifference to my feelings, I walked away, crushed and helplessly defeated. That night, I cried myself to sleep, still holding my broken doll. I hoped my mother would change her mind, but she never did. I remember mourning that doll for a long time and often stopped at the store where we had bought it. I would stand at the window, looking at the doll longingly, wishing to have such a doll again. For many years, I continued to look for her. Whenever I saw a doll store, I would look for a baby doll with the porcelain head and eyes that opened and closed.

One afternoon, many years later and after my own children were grown, I was on my way to the Lincoln Center in New York City to meet my husband. I passed a store selling dolls on Fifty-Seventh Street called The Magnificent Doll. To my amazement, it had such a doll, dressed in a long organdy dress, with a bonnet trimmed with lace, just as I remembered.

Without hesitation, I walked into the store, ready to buy the doll, but then thought it would not be a good idea to take her to the theater with me. I explained the situation to the saleslady, who had taken the doll out of the display window, and offered to leave a deposit, but was told that it was not necessary, and they would be glad to hold her for me. When I did come back, the doll was gone. The saleslady apologized and explained that another salesperson had sold it on her day off. When she saw how terribly disappointed I was, she said she could order another doll just like it from the Amish in Pennsylvania, and would call me as soon as it arrived, which she did.

Holding in my arms the doll I had longed for so many years earlier finally healed that painful childhood memory.

GETTING RESETTLED

While we were still in Poland, my father started a new business in Berlin, which was mainly a men's clothing store, but also carried work clothes and luggage. The apartment he rented was conveniently located across the street from the store so that my mother would be able to help him in their business. They registered Willi at the Kaiserstrasse Jewish Boys' School, and me at the Maedchen Volkschule on Auguststrasse. These boys' and girls' elementary schools were built and sponsored by the Berlin Jewish community.[20] In view of mounting antisemitism, Jewish community leaders foresaw the need for such schools and started them as early as 1929. They were equipped with the most modern facilities and staffed by outstanding educators.

Fanny's school, the Maedchen Volkschule on Auguststrasse

20 In the last few years of the Weimar Republic, even before Hitler's rise to power, antisemitism in Germany gathered strength and became a principal issue in the national political struggle to defeat democratic governance. Surging antisemitism and the German Jews' compromised economic situation and personal safety prompted them to reexamine their Jewish identity and seek new ways of sustaining community life.

The summer months were still ahead, and Willi and I would have time to get acquainted with children in our neighborhood. A Jewish family in our apartment building had a daughter my age and we became good friends. Her name was Gisela, but we called her Gisi. We were going to attend the same school in the fall and hoped to be in the same class. Gisi told me about the *Zuckertüte,* a colorful cardboard cone filled by friends and family with all kinds of candy to make the first day of school sweet, which I too would get. I was somewhat apprehensive about starting school, but hearing about the candy-filled cone, I actually looked forward to my first day there.

The day before school was scheduled to start, my mother and I went together to buy a *Zuckertüte.* That evening, Aunt Hella came especially to see me and brought a box of chocolates to add to my already full cone. I remember examining all the candies I had and carefully planning which to eat first and which to share with my brother. I felt bad for Willi because he was not going to get a *Zuckertüte,* since he was not starting first grade as he had already completed two years of school in Poland.

The next morning, I got up earlier than usual and called my mother to help me get dressed. My clothes had been carefully laid out on the chair next to my new leather school bag. When I was dressed and ready to leave, I proudly slipped my schoolbag onto my back and smelled the pungent odor of leather, which ever since reminds me of those first days of school. I held my mother's hand tightly as we approached the school and felt my heart beating faster when I saw all the strange new faces.

Our teacher, who directed us to an area where my classmates were waiting, welcomed us. I said goodbye to my mother, trying hard not to cry. When all the girls in my class were assembled, our teacher led us to our classroom where we were told to sit in alphabetical order. Since my last name started with "B," I found myself sitting in the first row, facing the teacher's desk. After taking attendance, our teacher, Fraulein Lichtenstein, introduced herself and proceeded to tell us about all the rules we would have to follow. "Every morning, when your teacher enters the classroom," she began, "you must stand up and say 'Good morning,' and then you may sit down. It is important that you remember to always sit up straight, with your hands clasped behind your chair."

Several years later, while absorbed in a story my teacher was telling us, I momentarily forgot that rule, releasing my hands from behind the chair.

I was leaning forward on my desk, listening intently, when I suddenly heard my name called out and was told to go to the principal's office. At first, I could not figure out what I had done, but then realized the "terrible crime" I had committed by releasing my hands from behind my chair.

On the first day of school, we were dismissed early. Our maid, Anna, was waiting for me, holding my candy cone. She had come to take me to the photographers, to have my picture taken to mark my first day at school. It was an unusually warm day for September and the woolen dress I was wearing felt hot and itchy so I did not look very happy in the photo. After the first day, my mother never walked me to school again. Since Gisi's mother walked her to school every day, my mother asked her if I could go with them. I would have liked my mother to take me to school like other mothers did, but she said it was a waste of time if Gisi's mother was willing to take me.

Fanny with *Zuckertüte*

I loved school, and although I was shy, I made friends quickly. All of our teachers were young Jewish women born in Germany. I soon discovered that most of the teachers favored the German-born children over those from Poland. One day, when I was in fourth grade, our class lined up to hand in our homework. The girl in front of me gave in her paper with a grease stain on it. I was next in line, and after the girl had left, I heard Fraulein Lichtenstein remark with disgust to a teacher standing next to her, "*Ost Juden*,[21] what can you expect?" I felt as though she had struck me. I could not believe that a Jewish teacher was prejudiced against her own people. That incident haunted me for many years, and left me wanting to prove to my teacher that, despite being born in Poland, I could live up to her high standards.

LEFT WITH STRANGERS, AGAIN

A few months after we had moved from Poland to Germany, my mother took my brother and me on a long trolley ride to the suburbs of Berlin. She had not told us anything about where we were going or why. We got off at the last stop, Heiligensee, which was in a deserted area. I remember seeing a cemetery in the distance, but we did not go in that direction. Straight ahead of us, we saw some tents. My mother walked toward them, with Willi and I following closely behind. As we came closer, I realized it was an outdoor flea market. I could not help but wonder why we had gone there, but did not want to ask any questions. I sensed that my mother was not in the mood for conversation.

Once inside the flea market, my mother approached a woman arranging wares on a table. A man, whom I assumed was her husband, was busy with a customer nearby. I overheard my mother asking the woman if she would watch my brother and me for a short time, explaining that she had an errand to run and could not take us with her. Willi and I looked at each other, dumbfounded, not knowing what to make of our mother's unexpected decision to leave us there. Surprised by our mother's request, the woman looked us over curiously, but then reluctantly agreed to watch us. Before we had a chance to object, Mother was gone. She walked away without even saying goodbye to us. There

21   Jews from Eastern Europe.

was nothing we could have done, short of creating a scene. So we sat down on a nearby bench and waited for our mother's return, hoping she would not be long.

I then remembered a similar situation when my mother had left me with a neighbor, when I was about four years old and we were still living in Poland (see *Left with Strangers*, p. 44). This time, at least, I was not alone, but was comforted by Willi's presence.

Willi and I sat quietly on that bench for a long time, waiting anxiously for our mother. We noticed that the people we were left with were whispering to each other, probably wondering why my mother had not yet returned. It might have been around lunchtime because the woman started to unwrap her sandwiches. She asked if we wanted something to eat, but before I could answer her, Willi poked me in the ribs and whispered urgently, "Tell her no thank you." So I did, and the woman said, "Let me know if you change your minds." Then, she sat down and began to eat. When I asked Willi why he told me that, he said, "The sandwiches may have ham in them, which we are not allowed to eat." "Oh," I said, "I'm glad you reminded me."

Another hour passed and I was becoming frantic. Some frightening thoughts ran through my mind. "What if my mother is not coming back? What if she got lost and can't find her way back to the flea market to pick us up? What will we do?" Willi must have been thinking the same thoughts. He was now swinging his legs back and forth, something he always did when he was upset. Yet, he still did not say anything to me, not wanting to frighten me more than I already was. I had a hard time suppressing my impulse to cry, but knew that would clearly give away how worried I really was. It was very difficult, but I had to control myself, if only for Willi's sake. He had enough to deal with, worrying about our mother's return and trying to figure out what to do if she did not come back.

The sun was about to go down. I tried to think reasonably. "Something must have happened to her. She would not leave us here for so long." The couple my mother had left us with started to pack up their things, then walked over to where we were sitting and asked us what our names were, and where we lived.

Just then, my mother appeared out of nowhere. She briefly thanked the man and woman, and told us to follow her. I wanted to ask my mother where she had been for so long, but I was so relieved to see her that I did not say anything. Willi did not say anything either, and did not even look at her. He was so angry about what she had put us through.

We walked to the trolley stop and boarded the trolley. My mother paid the fare and we sat down. Willi walked to the back of the vehicle and sat by himself. I still did not want to ask my mother anything about where she had been or why it had taken her so long. I was just pleased she had come back and we were finally going home.

Many years later, when I remembered the incident, I asked my mother why she had taken us to Heiligensee and left us for many hours with strangers at a flea market. She claimed she did not recollect ever taking us there, and I left it at that.

A CLOSE CALL

Almost two years had passed since we had immigrated to Germany in 1930. We started to experience some antisemitism, but life for me, as a seven-year-old, seemed relatively normal. My parents' business was thriving and they were not yet aware that the political situation was changing rapidly.

Regina and Lazer (Leo), in front of their uniform and clothing store in Berlin

Since our store was closed on Sundays, it gave our family a chance to spend some time together. We would go to Grunewald, a park in the Berlin suburbs, where we would picnic and enjoy the countryside, away from the city. When the weather was warm enough in July, we would often meet Aunt Hella and her family in Wannsee. Mutual friends of my parents and my aunt often joined us. The men would play cards under the shade of an umbrella, while the women sat nearby, engaged in conversation.

Fanny, Willi, and cousin Salo in Wannsee

On one of those Sundays, when we were all enjoying a day in the sun, Willi, my four-year-old cousin Salo, and I were playing in the sand near the water. We were building sand castles, digging moats around them, and filling them with water. I was the water carrier, and while filling my pail with water, I noticed a woman floating leisurely on an inner tube. I thought it would be great if I could float like that. I returned the pail to Willi and Salo and ran to my mother. I told her about the woman and begged her to ask the woman if she would take me for a ride. While annoyed at the interruption, my mother agreed to ask her. She followed me to the lake and waved to the woman on the tube to get her attention, who soon realized that we were trying to signal her to come closer. When she was within earshot, my mother asked her if she would give me a ride. The woman smiled and said, "Sure, hop on." My mother helped me get onto the woman's lap and left. I was very uncomfortable and when I tried to find a better position, we lost our balance and capsized. I sank into the water, noticing how green it was. Then, as I was about to black out, I felt a strong pull on my arm. When I came to, I was lying on the beach, surrounded by a crowd of people.

Willi had noticed the commotion on the beach and went to see what was going on. To his surprise, he saw me lying on the ground with a lifeguard attending to me. Frightened, my brother ran to tell our mother. I was still on the ground, coughing up water, when my mother arrived. Anxious and out of breath, she told the lifeguard that she was my mother and asked him if I was all right. Assuring her that I was, he said that I had gotten rid of all the water in my lungs. My mother thanked him profusely, then picked me up and carried me back to where we were sitting.

While wiping me dry, she started blaming me for what had happened. Aunt Hella, who overheard my mother, came to my defense. She was shocked that my mother was scolding me when I was so visibly shaken. "I can't believe that you are trying to blame Fanny," Aunt Hella said, obviously quite angry with her sister. "It was really your fault for allowing her to go on the inner tube with that woman. She is only a child and thought it would be fun. You can thank your lucky stars that she didn't drown." Realizing how harsh she had been with me, my mother stopped scolding me. After Aunt Hella left, my mother barely spoke, but she did say, "Stay here with me and don't go near the water any more."

My father had been so involved in his card game, he was unaware of what had happened. I doubt if my mother ever told him about my close call. If she had, he would have given her a good piece of his mind for letting me go on an inner tube with a total stranger.

As a rule, my father rarely went on these outings if Aunt Hella was going to be there. Whenever we did get together, I could not help noticing that my aunt and my father never spoke to each other. I thought about it again, seeing my aunt and my father at the beach that day, and a few days later I asked my mother if they were angry with each other. At first, she tried to evade the subject by telling me that they had some sort of misunderstanding, but I insisted, asking her to explain what the problem was. I loved both my aunt and my father and did not want there to be any bad feelings between them.

"You may not remember," my mother said, "but a few days before we left Poland, I got a letter from Aunt Hella. She wrote something very upsetting about your father. I could not tell you about it at the time, but in that letter she told me that your father had been spending his evenings playing cards and gambling. I was very upset and confronted your father and asked him if it was true. 'Yes, it's true,' he said. 'After working all day in the store, I needed some diversion and joined a group of men to play cards. What is wrong with that? Your sister had to make a big deal of it and write to you about it while you were still in Poland? All she accomplished was to drive a wedge between us and putting doubts in your mind about me.' After I heard your father's side of the story, I agreed with him. Aunt Hella had no business gossiping about your father to me, especially while I was still in Poland. She may have thought she was doing me a favor; instead, she alienated herself from your father and now he wants nothing to do with her."

I was surprised at Aunt Hella for doing such a thing, and I could not really blame my father for being angry. As young as I was, I was sure my father would not forgive Aunt Hella for what she had done. I was right; he never did.

HITLER'S RISE TO POWER

In 1932, about a year before Hitler was elected as the Reich's Chancellor, the Nazi Party won the election and the aging Von Hindenburg, a First World War hero, had no choice but to turn over the leadership to him.[22] Despite Hitler's resounding victory, many people felt it was a passing phase. They believed that the German people were not going to accept a madman like Hitler as their leader. After all, Germany, a cultured country, had given the world Mozart, Beethoven, Goethe, and Schiller, to name but a few. They thought it would blow over. But Germany, still in the throes of the Depression, was desperate for change. Hitler promised that he would lead them to prosperity. Pounding on the podium, and in a frenzy, I remember hearing him announce to the crowd that the first thing Germany must do is to make the country *Judenrein* (clean of Jews).

Carried away by Hitler's conviction, the German people hailed him as their new Führer. However, German Jews did not believe that Hitler was referring to them, as they assumed that when he said Germany must be made *Judenrein*, he does not mean them, since they were native-born Germans, but rather the *Ost Juden*. Shortly afterward, *Der Stürmer*, an official propagandist weekly,[23] started an aggressive campaign to demonize the Jews. They were depicted in comic strips as cheats and money-grubbers with thick lips and big noses; those malicious cartoons were conspicuously mounted in sealed glass cases on the outside walls of buildings all over Berlin.

Overnight, our neighbors began to resent us and treat us disdainfully. Some of the children living on our street made fun of and insulted me. One boy in particular took delight in repeatedly calling me a *dreckiger Jude* (dirty Jew). After a while, tired of being insulted, I warned him that, "The next time

22 Paul von Hindenburg (1847–1934) commanded the eastern front in the First World War. Respected for leading Germany to victory over Russia in the Battle of Tannenberg, he was appointed as the Chief of the General Staff. Elected President of the Weimar Republic in 1925, he painstakingly upheld the Republican constitution in his early years in office. At the age of eighty-five, Hindenburg ran again as a candidate for the presidency and was re-elected in 1932.

23 *Der Stürmer* was a radical antisemitic weekly magazine edited by Julius Streicher, a member of the National Socialist Party who ran a crude racist propaganda and incitement campaign against the Jews.

"The Day I Dared to be Defiant," Solarplate etching, 2002,
by Janet Lust Ganes, Fanny's daughter

you call me a dirty Jew, I am going to let you have it." He laughed it off, "*Ja, ja* (yes, yes), and what are you going to do about it?" "You just wait and see," I said, walking away.

A few days later, on the way back from our store to the apartment, the same boy and two of his friends blocked my way as I was trying to pass them. He sneered at me again, calling me a dirty Jew. Infuriated, I could not restrain myself any longer. Without warning, I pounced on him like a wildcat, grabbed his shirt and punched him in the face with such fury that I knocked out one of his teeth. He was so stunned that he did not even attempt to hit me back. His friends just stood there in shock, watching this little seven-year-old girl beat up their much taller friend. When the boy realized he was bleeding, he ran home crying and his friends left!

Out of breath, but pleased that I had retaliated, I ran back to our store and told my mother what had happened. She told me to go to the store's backroom and stay there, afraid the boy's parents might come looking for me. Within minutes, the boy's father rushed into our store, yelling, "Where is that brat? She knocked my son's tooth out."

Our tailor, Mr. Schimanski, who was doing alterations in back, heard the commotion and came out holding up a large pair of scissors and threatened the boy's father, "If you don't leave immediately, I am calling the police." Intimidated, Herr Duemmel backed out of the store, mumbling that he would get me another time. From my hiding place, I overheard what happened, and breathed a sigh of relief when the man left. For the next few days, I stayed out of sight and someone accompanied me whenever I left the house. Word must have gotten around, because I was never called a dirty Jew again.

MY FRIEND IRMA

During Hitler's regime, I had only one non-Jewish friend. Irma lived in the apartment house across the street from us. While I do not recall how our friendship started, I remember she had some sort of medical condition, which at times forced her to stay indoors. Her mother approached me one day and asked me if I would like to come to their house to play with her daughter. She briefly explained that Irma could not come out to play, but her condition was not contagious. I checked with my mother, who said that I could go.

Irma, an only child, was older than me. She had her own playroom, and the first time I walked into it, it felt like entering a toy store. One wall had built-in wooden shelves with many cubbyholes holding at least twenty-five dolls dressed in different outfits. Their hair was real and could be combed. It was hard for me to make up my mind which doll I wanted to play with. In the middle of the room, I saw a small-sized table set for a tea party with tiny porcelain dishes. Around the table were various stuffed animals on chairs, as if they were waiting for the party to begin. One teddy bear even had a bib tied under his chin. I stood there, fascinated, taking in the whole scene. I asked Irma how she was able to decide which toy or doll she would play with. "Oh, I take turns to make sure I play with each of them at some time or other. I don't want them to be jealous and get angry with me." "If I had such a playroom, I would never go out to play," I said. Irma just smiled and I could see that she was pleased.

Fanny and Irma in Berlin, 1933, before Irma joined the Hitler Youth

What I liked about her was that she never limited the toys I could play with, giving me free reign to pick and choose. Irma and I would play side by side for several hours at a time, never disagreeing about anything.

When Irma was about eleven years old, she joined the Hitler Youth,[24] and since I was Jewish, we had to part company. I realized that she had to do what was expected of her, and I did not hold it against her. Still, when I saw her in uniform for the first time, with the red armband bearing the black swastika, it gave me a jolt. She was up front, carrying the German flag. For a moment, I forgot myself, and waved to her. She quickly averted her eyes, afraid to acknowledge that she had associated with a Jew. I realized that she had to distance herself from me for her own protection, and I did not take it personally. Our friendship had come to an end because of harsh circumstances beyond our control.

A DISAPPOINTMENT

When I was about eight or nine years old, it became apparent to me that there was something lacking in my relationship with my mother. She showed little interest in what I was doing or who my friends were. She was also inconsistent in her behavior toward me and I never knew what to expect. Sometimes she made my lunch for school, but most of the time I had to make it myself. Several times a year, she would take me to a department store to buy me clothes for school. She made all the selections, and would not let me choose the clothes I liked. Those shopping trips usually turned out to be very unpleasant and I always ended up crying.

There was a leather jacket I wanted. Like today's denim jackets, they were the latest rage and most of my friends had them. When I asked my mother if she would buy me one, she said, "They are not very feminine and are more suited for boys, not girls." No amount of begging or pleading would change my mother's mind. It was just like the time my favorite doll broke and

---

24   The National Socialist youth movement (*Hitlerjugend*), which included most youth movements operating in Germany at the time, was led by Baldur von Schirach. According to legislation passed on December 1, 1936, membership in the *Hitlerjugend* was compulsory for youngsters aged ten to eighteen.

my mother refused to replace it. There was a heartlessness about her I never understood. I often wondered why she was like that.

In third grade, I realized that I had a natural ability for drawing, recognized by my art teacher as well as my classmates. Encouraged by this, I decided to take my folder of drawings home and show them to my mother. "How do you like my drawings?" I asked her. "I guess they are all right," she managed to say, totally devoid of enthusiasm or praise. Angry at her response, I closed my folder and said, "How come you never have anything nice to say about me or what I do?" Surprised at the confrontation, she was taken aback, but soon recovered, "Parents should not praise their children, or it will go to their heads," she said. "Even if they deserve to be praised?" I challenged. "Yes, even if they deserve it." She always justified herself, and, after a while, I avoided any disagreements with her, because I would always end up losing, and she would never admit that she could possibly be wrong.

She often reminded me how lucky I was to have a mother. "You can't imagine how much I suffered growing up with a stepmother," she would say to me time and again. I felt as if she envied me for having a mother, but in reality, I did not feel as lucky as she thought I should.

A VISIT TO HUNGARY

In the summer of 1936, when the Olympic Games were being held in Berlin,[25] our parents sent Willi and me to Hungary to visit my mother's youngest sister, Frieda. We would be traveling for many hours without any adult supervision and I had to rely on Willi to watch over me. We were surprised that our parents were willing to send us on that trip by ourselves, unsupervised, but my mother thought it would be a good experience for both of us. My father relied on my mother's judgment and would not oppose her, as was often the case. It seemed to me as if we were embarking on an adventure, especially

25 Before the 1936 Olympic Games in Munich, the Reich somewhat reduced the public mistreatment of Jews, giving them and the world the illusion that life under Nazi rule was possible.

since I had just read *Emil and the Detectives*.[26] We were also looking forward to meeting my mother's brother, Leo, about whom we had heard a great deal. We had our own passports, and arrangements were made with our uncle to meet us in Vienna, where we stopped over before going on to Hungary. After spending the night at Uncle Leo's house, in the morning we were put on the train bound for Hungary, where Aunt Frieda would be waiting for us.

Aunt Frieda and her sons Georg and Franzie, before they were taken to Auschwitz, c. 1942

Aunt Frieda and her husband Miklos lived in a spacious U-shaped house in the town of Tata.[27] Their living quarters were divided into separate wings. The house, enclosed by a wall, had a big yard, where we played with our cousins, Franzie and Georg. After living only in apartments until then, being in their house was a new experience for us.

26   A children's book by Erich Kästner, published in 1929, with a realistic plot, set in Berlin. The book was on the Nazis' blacklist of forbidden books.

27   An ancient fortress city in northwestern Hungary, on the crossroads between Vienna and Budapest, seventy kilometers from the latter. There was a village near Tata named Tovaros, and in 1938 the two were united under the name Tatatovaros. Later on they were once again separated and since 1954 the town has been known as Tata.

Before we left for our trip to Hungary, Willi suggested we bring a present for our cousins. The gift was a unique scooter, which was the latest rage in Berlin at that time. It had an extra board, which had to be pushed up and down with both feet, like a seesaw, to make it go. It had a gear attached to the rear wheel, and two hand brakes on the handlebars so it could be stopped safely before getting off. When Georg heard that we were bringing him the scooter, he refused to go to camp, and wanted to wait and see it.

Aunt Frieda owned a ladies clothing store in Tovaros and her husband owned a dry goods store next to their house. Every morning my aunt left after breakfast to go to Tovaros, while Willi and I, together with our cousins, were left in the nanny's care.

After Willi and I settled in and updated our aunt on our life in Germany, she was surprised to hear that neither Willi nor I knew how to swim. "We have got to do something about that," she said, and made arrangements for us to take swimming lessons. My aunt and uncle belonged to a community club in a nearby park, which had a swimming pool on the premises, with a lifeguard who could give us swimming lessons. Every morning the nanny walked us to the park, together with our cousins, for our swimming lessons. While we had lunch the nanny brought for us, we listened to the most enchanting music played by gypsy violinists. After lunch, we played in the park with our cousins for a while longer, chasing butterflies and trying to catch frogs. We returned home in time for dinner, with the family gathering in the dining room where the cook would serve our meals. We were introduced to vegetables we had never had before, which we ate with relish, but we looked forward most to the wonderful cakes the cook prepared each day for dessert. During dinner, each of us took turns telling our aunt and uncle about our day.

Every evening, after Franzie had his bath and was tucked into bed, I told him stories I had read. He never tired of hearing them and I had to talk till my mouth was hurting, otherwise he would not let me stop. This was how we spent most days of the week.

On weekends, Aunt Frieda took us on outings. We climbed mountains and picnicked at a nearby lake. Sometimes Aunt Frieda's friends came over with their children or nephews and nieces who were visiting them. Fortunately for us, everyone spoke German.

Fanny and Willi with cousin Franzie and friends

When we returned home, my mother asked me how I liked it at Aunt Frieda's. I started crying and told her I wished we could have stayed there. My mother was taken aback — it must have been unpleasant for her to hear that I was not happy to be home.

* * *

After our return, Willi celebrated his Bar Mitzvah at the local synagogue on Kleine Hamburger Strasse, where we went for Sabbath and holiday services. Willi read the weekly Torah (Bible) portion in Hebrew, and the rabbi and congregants congratulated him on his outstanding performance. He beamed as he shook hands with his friends and guests, wearing his *tallit* (prayer shawl) and blue high-school cap.

When the service at the synagogue was over, Willi's friends and other guests were invited to our home to partake of cakes baked by my mother at a buffet set up in our dining room. I remember Martin, his best friend, patting Willi on the back and saying, "Well done, Biene," (bee, in German) as his friends always called him, a nickname derived from our family name, Bienenfeld. I had never seen Willi looking so pleased, and was proud to be his sister.

Willi at his Bar Mitzvah, 1936

LIVING UNDER HITLER'S REGIME

In the years after my confrontation with the Nazi boy, life for Jews in Berlin became increasingly difficult as the Nuremberg laws[28] came into effect. Signs reading "Jews Not Admitted," were put up at movie ticket booths and elsewhere. Jews were forbidden to use most park benches, unless otherwise delineated. Those tactics were meant to segregate and humiliate us. I never sat on any of the benches in the park nor would I go to the movies, where I would have to pretend I was not Jewish.

I only associated with my friends from school and concentrated on my studies. I was now in seventh grade, studying German literature. Our class was given an assignment to select a poem by Friedrich Schiller,[29] learn it by heart, and recite it in class. Schiller was a favorite poet of mine. I found his work sensitive, inspiring, and beautifully rhymed. I chose *The Alpine Hunter,* a poem that tells the story of a youth who relentlessly pursues a gazelle. When my turn came, I recited the poem with great emotion. It reaches its climax when the youth corners the frightened animal and is about to release his arrow.

> …When from out the clefts behold
> Steps the mountains' genius old
> With his hands the deity
> Shields the breast that trembling sighs
> Must though even up to me
> Death and anguish send, he cries
> Earth has room for all to dwell
> Why pursue my loved gazelle?

28   The Nuremberg laws were enacted in September 1935, including the Reich Citizenship law, which deprived Jews of German citizenship, and the Law for the Protection of German Blood and German Honor, which forbade intermarriage between Jews and Germans. These statutes formed the basis for the exclusion of Jews from all areas of life in Germany and the advancement of the anti-Jewish policy.

29   Friedrich Schiller, a German poet and author (1759–1805), was the leader of the Romantic Movement.

Totally absorbed in reciting the poem, I had forgotten where I was and felt like I had taken my class up to the cliffs where the trembling animal stood frozen with fright. Then I heard a sigh of relief from my classmates, when the hermit appeared just in time to save the gazelle. I was rewarded with a resounding "Very good, Fanny," from my teacher and got an "A."

* * *

Shortly after the Nazis came to power, they began carrying out policies that would encourage Jews to leave Germany.[30] Many Jews, foreseeing the impending danger, liquidated their businesses and sold their homes. Others applied for papers to immigrate to the U.S.A., or fled to neighboring countries such as Belgium and France. Those leaving were only permitted to take out limited funds. Many found ways of taking their money out illegally or transferring their assets to Switzerland.

Some parents who were uncertain of whether they would be able to get out of Germany sent their children to England on the Kindertransport program.[31] Others left for Mandatory Palestine or countries such as Sweden and Denmark that agreed to take in many children. My brother's best friend, Martin, and his sister, Helga, were sent to England on the Kindertransport. Their parents hoped that if they could not get out, at least their children would survive. My parents never considered sending us away separately; my mother strongly believed that breaking up the family was not an option. My father had great confidence in my mother and supported her decision not to send us away.

A classmate of mine, Susie, was sent to live with a Jewish family in Denmark until she was able to immigrate to the Land of Israel. Her older

30   In the second half of 1937, a plan was implemented to expel Jews, employing the informal means of Aryanization (transfer of businesses to German ownership), and pressure designed to force Jews to emigrate.

31   Strenuous efforts were made to spare Jewish children from the impact of Nazi Germany's antisemitic laws on their lives. The Kristallnacht pogrom, in which hundreds of synagogues and thousands of Jewish-owned businesses across Germany were set ablaze and Jews were murdered and subjected to physical assault, provided the impetus for accelerating the child rescue activity. Under the Youth Aliyah program, adolescents were repatriated to pre-state Israel and the Inter-Aid Committee for Children transferred thousands of children, mostly to Britain, through the Kindertransport operation.

sister, Friedel, left a year earlier and was living on a kibbutz near Haifa, where Susie was hoping to join her.

Fanny's friend Susie, after arriving in the Land of Israel

As part of the hosting program, Susie would receive a bicycle to help her get around while living in Denmark. When she was notified that her bicycle was waiting for her at the Danish consulate, I offered to go and collect it with her. I would take my brother's bike on the train, and we would both ride home together on our bikes. Afraid that my mother would not give me permission to go, I did not tell her about our plan. I expected to be back before I was missed, but the trip back took much longer than I had anticipated. Both Susie and I were unfamiliar with that part of Berlin, and we had to stop many times to ask for directions.

When I finally got home, my mother was frantic. "Where have you been?" she asked. "We were looking all over for you. We didn't know where you were. I was terribly worried and was just about to call the police." I had never seen my mother so upset, except when Willi had his accident while crossing the street to buy me candy. I tried to explain myself and apologized for worrying her. "I'm sorry I didn't tell you, but Susie had to pick up her bike from the Danish consulate and I offered to accompany her. I had no idea it was going to take us so long." "You mean to tell me you rode all the way from the west side of Berlin on your bikes?" said my mother, sounding horrified. "We were very careful. We walked with our bikes across the intersections and rode them only on the sidewalks." My mother's expression softened from anger to relief. As upset as she was, she was thankful that I was unharmed. I could not blame her for being angry with me. I knew only too well how she must have felt. It reminded me of the time my mother had left Willi and me at the flea market for an afternoon that had seemed like eternity. Not knowing whether you will ever again see someone you really love is frightening. If nothing else, that incident proved that perhaps I had misjudged my mother's feelings for me. She cared about me more than she showed.

* * *

In 1937, my friend Gisi was the first of my close friends to leave Germany. Relatives had sent her family affidavits to immigrate to the U.S.A. As the political situation worsened, my mother contacted her sisters, Helen and Clara, in New York, and asked them to start working on papers for us so that we, too, would be able to immigrate to the U.S.A.

The apartment building where we lived seemed to have become a transit point for Jews leaving Germany. A young couple by the name of Finkelstein moved into our building for a short time with their one-year-old son, Peter. As I was always very fond of children, I often went to their house to play with little Peter. Within a few months they left for Shanghai, one of the few escape routes for Jews not requiring visas or entry papers.

Our classes in school were thinning out as more and more Jews left Germany. My teacher of four years, Freulein Lichtenstein, left for the Land of Israel. She was lucky to have a place to go because she had a brother there. My new teacher, Freulein Bergas, could have left as well, but she had an elderly mother, whom she did not want to leave behind in an old age home.

In 1937, while the papers we needed for immigration to the U.S.A. were being processed, the rumors of an impending war were mounting. Nonetheless, that year I went to Poland by myself for the summer to visit my grandfather, and was looking forward to seeing Cesia again, who was living near him.

Visiting in Poland, 1937; Fanny and Willi with Grandfather, Cesia, and Salo, Samusch, Aunt Reshka, Uncle Leo, and Aunt Hella

When I returned to Germany, not much had changed on the surface, although we heard that some people had been taken to work camps.

RETURNING TO POLAND

On November 8, 1938, we were tipped off by a customer at our store, who was an SS officer, about a raid to arrest and deport all Jews of foreign origin. He advised my parents not to stay at home that night.[32] We passed on the information to as many of our friends and family as we

32   The deportation of some 15,000 Jews of Polish nationality began in October 1938.

could, and asked a Christian couple we knew and could trust to hide us overnight. They agreed to have us stay at their home at great risk, and we spent a sleepless night on the outskirts of Berlin. The raid later became known as the infamous Kristallnacht.[33] Jewish people finally realized that staying in Germany any longer would be dangerous.

Upon returning to our apartment the next day, we were surprised to see everything intact. Our store had not been vandalized, and the windows were not broken. The only damage was a large sign, *Jude*, painted on our display window in a garish yellow. We never forgot the people who hid us on Kristallnacht. In gratitude, my mother sent them care packages for many years after the war.

After that night, life in Berlin became even more difficult for us. My parents decided that we could not risk staying in Germany any longer. Since we were Polish citizens, we could return to Poland and wait there for our visas to immigrate to the U.S.A. Unfortunately, the Polish quota was very full and we had no way of knowing how long we would have to wait to get our visas. My parents started to liquidate the inventory in our store and sold most of our personal belongings. Within a few months, we were ready to leave Germany. Although I was pleased about it, it was hard for me to say goodbye to my friends and leave the school I loved. I realized then that the carefree days of my childhood had come to an end. At the beginning of August 1939, when we finally left Germany, I was about to turn fourteen.

Since there was an American consulate in Kraków, my parents decided to go there, instead of to Tarnów where we lived before moving to Germany. We managed to rent an apartment from someone who later turned out to be an antisemite.

There were still several weeks of summer left, and since there was nothing of interest for me to do in Kraków, I begged my parents to let me go back to

---

33   After the German diplomat, Ernst von Rath, was assassinated in Paris by a young Jew named Herschel Grynszpan, whose parents were among those deported from Germany to Poland and stranded in no man's land due to the Polish authorities' refusal to readmit them to Poland, the Nazis launched a pogrom known as Kristallnacht on November 9–10, 1938. On that night, the Nazis officially started the "War against the Jews" by breaking the windows of all Jewish stores and burning Jewish books and synagogues. The pogrom was not a spontaneous reaction to the assassination but a contingency plan prepared in advance.

Fanny, before leaving Germany in 1939

Tarnów. It was only two hours away by train and I could visit my grandparents, but, most of all, I wanted to spend the rest of the summer with my cousin, Cesia. Besides being cousins, Cesia and I had developed a special closeness in early childhood and had grown even closer because we spent the previous two summers together. I was overjoyed when my parents agreed to let me go, and, to save precious time, I packed my clothes quickly and left the next day.

Somehow I sensed that this might be my last visit with Cesia, and what a glorious few weeks we had together. We spent part of the time at my grandfather's country house in Zglobice, where we swam in the Dunajec River. We liked to sit under an old mulberry tree near his house and eat the sweet white fruit, talking endlessly about everything that had happened since we had last seen each other. Every afternoon, a farmer would deliver freshly picked wild strawberries, a wonderful treat that I never had in Germany.

My grandfather was an imposing man, with a long gray beard. He was religious, and stringently observed *kashrut* laws. We always had our meals together and my grandfather sat at the head of the table like a true patriarch.

My mother had told me many stories about meal-times at home when she was a child. My grandfather, then the father of a large brood of children, demanded decorum at the dinner table, and had his ways to ensure everyone behaved, as I mentioned earlier. Although my grandfather had many grandchildren, Cesia was the only one living nearby. Most of his grandchildren were scattered in other countries and did not visit him as often as I did. Knowing how much I liked swings, my grandfather had one built specially for me when I visited, which would be dismantled when I left. I remember him giving instructions to a peasant he hired to do this, and how he lost his patience and cursed under his breath when he could not make the man understand what he wanted done. I appreciated how much my grandfather went out of his way for me and will always cherish my memories of him.

My grandmother, Gittel, was an extraordinary cook. I am sure my grandfather married his third wife for her culinary talent. She was a short and surprisingly thin woman for someone who was such an excellent cook. While my mother told me many horror stories about her, I refused to see her through my mother's eyes. The only grandmother I had, she was wonderful to me. When we visited, she made special treats for us. My favorite was blueberry yeast pockets, still warm from the oven. She liked to watch us enjoying them and would laugh when we noticed that our lips and teeth had turned blue.

On Fridays, we were allowed to help prepare the Sabbath meals. The aromas from the kitchen made our mouths water and we could not wait for the evening meal. Many years later, I tried to make some of my grandmother's fantastic dishes, but to this day, I have not been able to duplicate her wonderful recipes. I suppose I am still trying to recapture the peaceful innocence of that time in my life. How could I ever forget the golden wheat fields sprinkled with red poppies and blue cornflowers? I can still hear the laughter ringing in my ears as Cesia and I ran through them, picking armfuls of flowers. Then, we would sit by the brook and weave them into garlands.

Cesia had a dog named Pikush who followed us everywhere. He was a great sport, and accepted our antics. Once, Cesia put sunglasses on him and tied a kerchief around his head to keep them in place. Pikush looked like an old lady sitting with us, content to amuse us. We would bring soda with us and give some to Pikush, who made us laugh as he cautiously lapped up the bubbly soda.

* * *

Back in Kraków, my parents were evicted from their apartment by their landlord who decided he no longer wanted Jewish refugees living in his building. Since Kraków already had a large influx of refugees, my parents had no choice but to move into an apartment shared with three other Jewish families. My brother, Willi, kept abreast of what was happening in the world by listening to a short-wave radio we brought with us from Germany. One morning, he heard that Poland was about to be invaded, and ran to notify my parents, who realized that I might be stranded in Tarnów. Concerned, my father left on the next train to bring me back home.

My grandparents and I were surprised by my father's sudden appearance, and shocked to hear of the impending invasion. While I was hurriedly getting my things together, we heard an explosion, which we later learned was a bomb that hit the Tarnów railroad station. Fortunately, there was no serious damage so my father and I were able to leave.

Cesia and I said a tearful goodbye, reminiscent of the one long ago. We clung to each other in a futile attempt to prolong our time together. We sensed that we might never see each other again. I continued to wave as the train pulled out of the station. Through my tears, I watched my cousin disappear into the distance. Not only was I saying goodbye to my cousin, but also to my childhood that had come to such an abrupt end.

When my father and I arrived in Kraków, there was utter chaos in the streets. There were crowds of people on the main roads, carrying bundles and suitcases, looking confused and distracted. Others were sitting atop horse-drawn wagons, their cattle hitched to the back, following closely behind. We made our way through the crowd to our apartment, where my mother and brother welcomed us home, relieved to see us safe and sound.

That night, Kraków was bombed.[34] When the warning siren sounded, everyone in our building was directed to the basement, which served as a bomb shelter. Most of the people were calm and followed instructions. It was crowded, but everyone managed to find a place on the dirt floor. It was a tense time. I heard some people asking God for forgiveness. Others prayed silently,

34 Later, on September 6, after a softening-up bombardment, German forces entered Kraków, one of Poland's oldest cities, the third-largest in size, and proclaimed it the capital of the Generalgouvernement — the general government zone — including large areas of occupied Poland (not including the areas in western Poland that were annexed to the Reich).

holding on to their rosary beads. Mothers tried to reassure their whimpering children. During the raid, we sat huddled together, terrified of the whistling bombs exploding around us. After what seemed like an eternity, the "all clear" sounded, and we thanked God for having been spared.

MY ACT OF BRAVERY

The next morning, September 1, 1939, Hitler's army marched into Poland. We watched them from our window when they marched into Kraków. As the jeeps and tanks rolled by, we noticed that some people waved to the German soldiers while others stood subdued on the sidewalk wondering about the fate awaiting them.

Shortly after the invasion, rumors of atrocities began to circulate. Jews were rounded up, arrested at random, and sent to work camps, and their families never saw or heard from them again. Those who resisted arrest were shot without mercy. To make things worse, the local Christian population cooperated with the Nazis, showing them the houses where Jews were living.

All the Jews in Kraków were issued yellow armbands featuring a blue Star of David, as well as yellow stars to be sewn onto their coats. We decided not to wear them since this would make us easy targets. Fortunately, we lived in a section of Kraków with not many Jews, and, therefore, we were not likely to be stopped. We stayed in our apartment where we felt safe, venturing out only when absolutely necessary. We still listened to our short-wave radio, our only contact with the outside world.

One day, my mother, my brother, and I were in the apartment. My father was not at home; I have no clear recollection of where he was. We heard heavy footsteps coming up the stairs and listened with apprehension, hoping they would pass by our door. But the footsteps grew louder and closer. We held our breath and realized, to our horror, that they had stopped at our door. There was a brief moment of silence followed by violent pounding, "Open up. Open the door. Gestapo." Frightened, we stood in the doorway of our room as Milsha, a young woman from one of the other families in the apartment, opened the door. A young man in uniform came in, holding a piece of paper. An older SS man followed closely behind. "Heil Hitler!" the first one said, extending his arm in salute and clicking his heels. "We have a report that one of you in this apartment has a short-wave radio. Which one of you is Bienenfeld?" "Here," my mother answered. We walked into our room with them and they closed the door. The older man searched the room and quickly found the radio, which was in plain sight. We watched anxiously to see what was going to happen next. At fourteen, I was unaware of how serious the situation was. After all, I thought, it is not a crime to own a radio. I glanced at my mother and was surprised to see that she looked frightened. A deathly silence filled the room.

The young SS man started pacing back and forth, somewhat ill at ease, and took off his gloves. Without looking at us, he finally said, "Your kind has taught us how to look for hidden gold. Undress," he ordered, pointing at my mother. "You too," he said, lifting his chin in my direction. "Machen Sie schnell!"[35] The officer had now stopped pacing and stood before us, legs astride, hitting his gloves impatiently against his hand. His partner put his revolver on the table and sat down. I looked at my mother and could not believe that she had actually started undressing. Outraged and embarrassed by the orders, my heart began to pound. I felt my face flush in anger. For a moment I forgot who I was and where I was. I faced the two Nazis, and, with measured breath, said in perfect German, "How dare you humiliate innocent people this way. In Germany, you were always models of good manners, and now you come here and do this? Shame on you!" I shouted, shaking in rage. My words echoed in the silence that followed. My mother gasped, "Fanny," staring at me in disbelief. My brother looked at me as if I had gone mad, but no one said a word.

Looks of surprise were clearly written on the two men's faces. "Ziehen Sie sich an (Get dressed)," I heard the young officer say quietly to my mother. Without another word, one of them picked up the radio, the other his revolver, and they left.

We listened to the descending footsteps. No one moved, and, for a moment, it seemed as if the world was standing still.

After the Gestapo had left, the families who shared the apartment with us told us they had braced themselves to hear a gunshot from our room, which thankfully, they never did.

---

35   Get on with it, fast.

PASSPORT TO FREEDOM

After the Gestapo searched our apartment, we lived in constant fear of hearing that dreadful pounding on our door again. There was no doubt in our minds that the Polish landlord, who had evicted us from our previous apartment, had reported us to them. Because of the arrests in the streets every day, my father and brother were now confined indoors. Without our short-wave radio, we felt isolated and shut off from the outside world.

A determined woman, my mother gathered as much information as she could about the possibility of escape. Almost every day, she would go out into the streets of Kraków to see if there was anything to learn. One day, as my mother approached the center of town, she saw that the streets were full of soldiers and officers standing in groups, laughing and talking. My mother was not afraid of the Germans. She had business dealings with them on a daily basis. Unfazed by the scene, she walked through the crowd, when suddenly she heard someone call her name. Surprised, she turned around to see who it was and recognized a former customer from our store in Berlin, now dressed in uniform. Surprised to see her, the officer said, "Frau Bienenfeld, what on earth are you doing in Poland?" Taken aback at being recognized, my mother did not know how to respond, but relaxed when she saw how friendly and genuinely interested the officer was. Encouraged by his sincerity, my mother told him about our situation. "We had to return to Poland," she explained, "and are waiting for our visas to immigrate to the U.S.A. Unfortunately, the Polish quota is very full and there is nothing we can do except wait." The officer listened with interest, and then asked my mother in which district of Kraków she lived. When she told him, he smiled and said, "Sie haben aber glück."[36] A good friend of mine is a colonel at the Gestapo headquarters. He is in charge of your district and I think he will be able to help you. Here is his name and address," he said, writing out the information on a piece of paper. "Go see my friend and tell him I sent you." My mother stared at the paper he had handed her and almost forgot to thank him. Then she heard him say, "Viel glück (Good luck)," as he waved goodbye.

When my mother recovered from what had just taken place, she could not wait to get home to tell us her incredible news. She was totally out of

---

36   You are in luck.

breath when she came in and had to sit in a chair to calm herself down. After regaining her composure, she told us about the unbelievable coincidence of meeting a former customer from our store who had recognized her on the street and had actually offered to help us. After listening to the whole story, we came to the conclusion that it must have been the hand of God that led my mother to that street.

Later that day, we all sat together to discuss how my mother should present our situation to the colonel, and realized that there was no way to prepare for such a meeting. My mother had one advantage in her favor. She spoke German fluently without a trace of an accent, which was very unusual for someone born in Poland. The morning that she was going to meet the colonel, my mother took great care in selecting her clothes. It was important to make a good impression. When she was dressed and ready to leave, we wished her good luck and agreed that she looked elegant. It was only a short walk from our apartment to the Nazi headquarters. As my mother approached the building and saw the red Nazi flags with their threatening black swastikas, her heart skipped a beat. Realizing the enormity of what she was about to do, she took a deep breath and said a prayer before knocking on the colonel's door.

An orderly looked surprised to see a woman asking to see his superior. He respectfully led her to the colonel's office and, after knocking, announced her presence, "Heil Hitler, Frau Bienenfeld is here to see you," he said, then closed the door behind him. The colonel rose from behind his desk and graciously asked my mother to sit down, curious to hear what had brought her to see him.

Somewhat nervous, my mother started to tell the colonel about meeting his friend, who had suggested that she go to see him. "We are about to leave for the U.S.A.," she explained, "and all our papers are ready. Unfortunately, we have to wait for our number to come up and there is no way of telling how long that will take. We arrived from Berlin only a few weeks ago and are now stranded here in Poland. You see," she added uneasily, "I am married to a Jewish man and have two children. Do you think you can help us?" she asked, looking hopefully at the colonel, then lost her courage and started to cry.

The colonel listened carefully and seemed surprisingly sympathetic. He was sitting at his desk, deliberating, while my mother dabbed at her tear-stained face. A few minutes later, he got up, and, as if he had just remembered something, said, "There are still some consulates open in Warsaw. I'm going to give you a travel permit. Leave for Warsaw as soon as you can. Take your passports with you and buy visas from any consulate outside Europe willing to sell them to you. Once the visas are stamped into your passports, you will be able to get transit visas to Italy." He then walked back to his desk, wrote something on a piece of paper, stamped it and handed it to my mother. He then wished her good luck, and led her to the door. When she got outside, my mother breathed a deep sigh of relief. The Nazi flags no longer looked as intimidating. The travel permit she now held in her hand could be our passport to freedom.

The next morning, my mother set out to follow the colonel's instructions. This time she got dressed like a peasant woman to blend in with the passengers on the train. She bought her ticket without any difficulty and boarded the train to Warsaw. However, it did not leave the station until a German soldier checked each compartment to see if there were any Jews aboard. He walked through the train shouting, "Alle Juden heraus,"[37] as he opened and closed the doors of each compartment. My mother's heart was pounding, even though she held the permit in her hand, and only after the soldier had checked and returned it to her was she able to relax.

When she arrived in Warsaw, she found several consulates still open. She decided to get visas to Honduras since it was the closest country to the U.S.A. Once the visas were stamped into our passports, there was no reason to delay her return and my mother boarded the next train back to Kraków. The trip back was uneventful and my mother had a chance to relax and go over the events of the last few days. Everything had happened so fast. She had been pleasantly surprised at the colonel's willingness to help her. Although he had not asked about her status, he probably assumed that my mother was an Aryan married to a Jew, and felt sorry for her. Soon after she returned, the transit visas to Italy were stamped into our passports and there was no longer any reason to delay our departure. We started packing and hoped to be out of Poland within a few days.

37   All Jews, get out.

A DESPERATE PLEA

We contacted our relatives in Tarnów and informed them that we were about to leave Poland. While we were packing, my mother's sister, Hella, and her husband, Josef, arrived unexpectedly to say goodbye. Both my uncle and aunt looked distraught, and Willi and I were surprised that they did not say hello to us. Our families had always been very close. Aunt Hella, especially, was like a second mother to us, and Willi and I had spent a lot of time with them and their son, Salo. Unfortunately, they failed to heed my mother's warning not to be home on Kristallnacht, when, at that time, they were living in Germany, and my Uncle Josef was arrested and sent back to Poland. My aunt had to liquidate their leather goods business, and, together with her son, followed my uncle to Poland. They were now living at my grandfather's house in Zglobice, not far from Tarnów, and were also waiting to immigrate to the U.S.A. When my aunt saw we were packing and almost ready to leave, she became frantic. She called my mother into an adjacent room, where Willi and I were at the time. At first, the two sisters were quietly engaged in conversation when suddenly we saw Aunt Hella drop to her knees in front of my mother, grab her hand and cry, "Regina, please take us with you. Don't leave without us! Please, please don't leave us here to die!"

My mother stood helpless, unable to console her sister. Willi and I were shocked to see our aunt, always so composed, react to our leaving in such a desperate way. Finally, my mother managed to say she would try to help her when we got to Italy, but in her heart she knew it was too late for them to get visas and enough money to fund their trip.

"Come, let's go," Uncle Josef said to my aunt, as he helped her up. They left, feeling hopeless and betrayed, without saying goodbye. Witnessing this scene haunted my family for the rest of our lives, especially my mother, who never forgave herself for not trying to help her sister. That was the last time we saw them. Sadly, after the war, we heard that my aunt, her husband, and their son had been murdered in Auschwitz.

Shortly after we arrived in Trieste, Italy, in January of 1940, both my hands broke out in a terrible rash that itched, making my skin peel. My mother took me to a doctor who could not tell us what it was, but suspected that it could have come about from some sort of emotional trauma. He bandaged my hands and prescribed a salve to soothe the pain. It took many weeks before my hands began to heal. The strangest part about this episode was that my Aunt Hella also had eczema on her hands for as long as I could remember, so she always wore white gloves when she prepared meals. It was uncanny that my distress was manifested in this way.

Many years later, when I was already a mother of two young boys, and expecting my third child, Aunt Hella appeared to me in a dream. I only saw her silhouette, but recognized her immediately. Her face was turned away as if she did not want me to see it, and I heard her say clearly and deliberately, "If not for you, my name will never be used." I knew what she meant; I was the only one left who could name a child after her. I then knew that I was going to have a girl, whom we named Chaya, my aunt's Hebrew name, which means life.

Aunt Hella

OUT OF POLAND AND IN TO ITALY

Our family was part of a transport of about 100 refugees who, like us, had miraculously found a way to get out of occupied Poland. Together, we left Kraków for Trieste, Italy. An attractive Polish woman named Marushka arranged the transport. She had an Italian boyfriend, a customs inspector at the border who was going to waive the transport through without inspection. Before we left Poland, she made it very clear to us that she expected compensation for her services. My mother gave her an onyx ring with a diamond in the center. When she found out that we had recently come from Germany, she asked my mother if, by any chance, she had a *knirps*.[38] We had one and it made Marushka very happy when my mother gave it to her. It was amazing to me that at a time when life seemed so uncertain, some people still felt the need for such a frivolous thing as a folding umbrella. Perhaps her way of holding on to life's little things made life feel normal, if only for a short time.

The border crossing was uneventful and we arrived safely in Trieste. There, we contacted HIAS.[39] They helped us find a place to live, provided us with breakfast coupons, and, ultimately, helped us get out of Europe.

We subleased a large room from a German widow, Mrs. Augscheller, who was a bit eccentric. She rented us the room only on condition that we would wear velvet pads with elastic bands that slipped easily over our shoes at all times so as not to scratch her beautiful parquet floors. It seemed ridiculous to us, but we had to abide by her rules. Willi and I tried to fool Mrs. Augscheller by not wearing the pads and see if she would know the difference, but our landlady was always listening. If she heard our footsteps, she would knock on the wall to remind us to put the pads on.

I was registered at an elementary school nearby, and was put in fourth, instead of eighth, grade. This was humiliating, as I could not understand what difference the grade I was in made if I could not understand the language. After a couple of weeks, I stopped going to school.

38 A folding umbrella that was a novelty at that time.
39 HIAS, the Hebrew Immigration Aid Society, was established in the U.S.A. in 1909. HIAS had branches in most European cities that were not occupied by Germany.

With a lot of time on my hands and nothing to do, I took daily walks all over the city. Once, I discovered a bookstore, and while browsing for some German books to read, I came across a series I had read in Germany called *Nesthaechen*. The books were about a young girl at different stages of her life, similar to *Anne of Green Gables*. The owner of the store was very kind, and, when he found out I was a refugee, loaned the books to me free of charge.

A few months later, I found a job as a companion to a seven-year-old Jewish boy named Franco. My job was to pick him up from school, bring him home for a snack, then either play with him at home or take him to the park. Franco understood but could not speak German. He taught me some Italian and we got along well. He lived in a large, beautifully appointed apartment in a wealthy section of Trieste. His mother was an attractive blonde woman with an aristocratic demeanor who spoke to me in fluent German.[40] Sometimes Franco's mother would ask us to meet her at the piazza and treat us to ice cream or pastries at an outdoor café.

After we were settled in, my mother realized that she should try to find her brother Max, who was in Naples, studying at university. Max was my mother's half-brother; he was the third child of four children born to Gittel, Psachye's third wife. Through HIAS, we were able to locate him, and he came to stay with us in Trieste. We were shocked to see that he was in terrible health. My mother made Max stay in bed and nursed him back to health, until he regained his strength. He was scheduled to leave for the Land of Israel in a few weeks and had to pass a physical examination before he could emigrate. Their oldest brother, Leo, had been financing Max's education, and after the war began, the two brothers lost contact with each other, and Max was left without any money.

Willi and I had never met Uncle Max, although we had heard a lot about him. Everyone in the family was very proud of him, as he was the only one with a college education. On our visits to our grandparents in Poland, Max was away in Italy, studying to be an agronomist. He had a wonderful sense of humor and always found something to joke about. When he first came to stay with us, he was so weak he could barely talk. A few weeks later, when he was feeling well again, it was good to hear him laugh and joke.

40   Trieste is located near the Austrian Alps, in an area where many people spoke German.

Taking care of her brother was very therapeutic for my mother. I think it helped soothe the pain of having to leave her sister behind. We did not talk about Aunt Hella after we left Poland; it was just too painful for all of us. We were preoccupied with trying to survive, worrying endlessly about whether we would ever reach our destination.

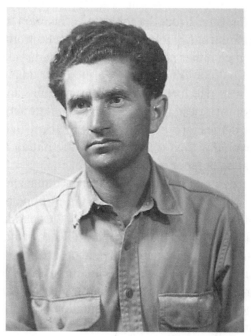

Uncle Max, after arriving in the Land of Israel

ON TO NORTH AFRICA

When Mussolini signed the Axis agreement with Hitler,[41] we knew we had to get out of Italy or risk being sent back to Poland. Alarmed, my mother made a brief trip to Naples to check with the American consulate on the status of the Polish quota. Unfortunately, there was no change in its status, and she returned to Trieste, very worried about our situation.

Concerned for the safety of the refugees in Trieste, HIAS was frantically trying to get them out of Italy. Their efforts were rewarded when they learned that there was a ship leaving Genoa bound for South America. HIAS convinced the captain to take aboard all the stranded refugees and make a stop in Tangier, North Africa, an international zone,[42] to allow the refugees to disembark there. The captain agreed, on condition that he was paid US $100 per person. The price was agreed upon and HIAS told us all to be ready to leave immediately. We packed our belongings as quickly as we could and left for Genoa by train.

Our group of refugees had developed camaraderie, and some people offered to pay the fares of those lacking sufficient funds. No one needed this at the time, but it was reassuring to have such caring people among us. Before we left Poland, we had to find a way to smuggle our money out, since this was illegal. My brother had a great idea: folding a large bill flat enough to slip behind the locks of our suitcases. One of my ideas was to push several large denomination American bills into a hollow ceramic candlestick. We could not have attempted to leave Poland without any money. There was no way to estimate how long the journey would take, and my parents were worried we would run out of money.

Since Tangier was an international free port, visas and entry papers were not required. Shanghai in China, Casablanca in Morocco, and Tangier in northern Morocco were the main escape routes from the war raging in Europe. After a pleasant two-day voyage, the *Conte Grande* docked safely in

41 The Axis agreement, signed in Berlin by Nazi Germany, Japan, and Fascist Italy on September 27, 1940, formalized the signatories' strategic partnership and the mutual recognition of each party's sphere of interests.

42 Tangier is a port city in northern Morocco overlooking the western entrance to the Straits of Gibraltar. Between 1923 and 1956, annexed to Morocco, it had international status, and was run by several European countries under a special accord.

Tangier harbor, and all the refugees from Trieste started to disembark. It was the first time we saw African natives, and we were very curious. At the dock, groups of five to six Arabs, barefoot, naked from the waist up, and wearing red pantaloons tight at the knee, with red cotton turbans wrapped around their heads, speaking loudly in Arabic, kept an eye on the disembarking passengers. Several donkeys stood nearby.

After we collected our luggage, a tall Arab appeared with his donkey. Without saying anything, he started loading our belongings into straw pouches slung across the donkey's back. We were terrified until we realized that it was some sort of taxi service. After he finished loading the luggage, he motioned to us to follow him. We had no idea where he was taking us, and had no choice but to comply. Afraid of losing sight of our worldly possessions, running after the Arab and his donkey, racing downhill, we must have been a comical sight indeed. After about ten minutes, we saw from a distance that the Arab had finally stopped in front of a hotel and was unloading our baggage on the sidewalk. When we caught up with him, he was waiting for us to pay him. He motioned to my father, and after a lot of gesturing, they finally agreed on a price. The Arab walked away, grumbling and counting his money, clearly unhappy with the sum he received. When he was out of sight, we all burst out laughing. I was not sure if we were laughing out of relief at not having lost our luggage or at the comical situation we had just experienced. It was among the lighter moments in our journey!

We arrived in Tangier on a bright afternoon in May. The sky was a deep blue, and, although it was hot, we felt a cool breeze coming off the ocean. As I looked up, I saw Tangier on a hill before me. The stucco houses, with their red tile roofs, looked as though they were stacked on top of each other and I wondered how it was possible to get to the top of the hill. I found it a mysterious place, as in the tales in *A Thousand and One Nights*.[43]

Most of the residents were multilingual, but school was taught in French. Since I had no knowledge of the language, I could not attend school, again. However, I had studied English for several years in Germany and was quite fluent. To reinforce my vocabulary, I went to the movies regularly.

The cost of living in Tangier was low and my father took advantage of the currency exchange rate to get the maximum francs for his dollars. My

---

43   *A Thousand and One Nights* is a collection of stories about the Arab world, originating in India, and first published in French, in the eighteenth century.

mother took in a boarder, a man from our refugee group, to supplement our income. My brother found a job as a dental assistant, thereby also earning some money. I managed to find a baby-sitting job for a five-year-old girl, also from our group. However, I did not have the same relationship with her as I had with Franco, even though we spoke the same language. It was a way of earning some spending money, so I made the best of the situation.

Fortunately, there was a girl of my age in our group, called Rutie. She too came from Poland and we became good friends. She could not attend school either, so we spent a lot of time together. We went to the beach almost every day and saw some of the latest American movies. Rutie was very good company and fun to be with. The summer was almost over and I needed to do something constructive. We found a dressmaker who took me on as an apprentice, and, although I did not get paid, it was valuable experience.

LEAVING TANGIER

There was an American consulate in Tangier, where we were able to check the status of the Polish quota periodically. In November 1940, President Roosevelt was elected for a third term. The consul in Tangier, elated by the Democratic Party victory, granted entry visas to the refugees on the waiting list.[44] The first to receive our visas, we had to prepare to leave once again.

Portugal was neutral during the Second World War, and Lisbon was the only port from which we could sail to the U.S.A. Since there were no direct flights from Tangier to Lisbon, we would have to fly to Seville, in Spain. This complicated matters enormously because we had to find a way to get from Seville to Lisbon.

At the airport in Tangier, we realized to our horror that we were scheduled to take a Lufthansa flight, the only commercial airline operating from there at that time. We were very uncomfortable about it, and it was strange for us to have to read our flight instructions in German.

---

44   After Kristallnacht, large-scale diplomatic activity was conducted in an attempt to find a solution to the refugee problem. The reelected Roosevelt government refrained from any involvement in Europe but held a positive attitude toward aiding refugees.

Seville seemed quaint and primitive to me. Only two years had passed since the Spanish Civil War[45] ended, and the poverty in the country was still apparent. I do not remember much about our stay there, except that I was attacked by hordes of bedbugs and could not sleep all that night. The next day, we were scheduled to take a ferry across the Tagus River, and then a train to Lisbon. However, there was no ferry when we arrived at the Tagus crossing point, only a makeshift raft whose boatman had a single oar. The boatman looked as if he was in dire straits, and we looked at one another, afraid to get on the raft. Suspecting our hesitance to get on board, the boatman quickly loaded our baggage. He then refused to take us across unless we agreed to pay more. We paid up, afraid of what he might do if we did not go along with this demands, or lest we risk being stranded in Seville. It was getting dark and we were the only ones on the dock. We reluctantly boarded the raft. It was a bitter cold December day, and I could not help noticing that the boatman's legs were wrapped in rags and he wore raffia sandals. I felt sorry for him, while my parents and brother were ill at ease and anxious to get to the other side. I have no recollection of what happened next, nor do I remember how we got to Lisbon. I must have slept through it all, after being awake the night before because of the bedbugs.

In Lisbon, we waited for the *Serpa Pinto*, the ship that would take us to our long-awaited destination, the U.S.A. Since our funds were low, we could only afford steerage for our transatlantic crossing. When we had been out at sea for several days, we encountered a terrible storm that left all the passengers very seasick. I remember feeling so sick that I was sure I would die. I swore that if I lived through this trip, I would never set foot on a ship again.

During the raging storm, the captain announced over the loudspeakers that both Hitler and Mussolini were dead, and the war was over. Of course it was not true; he was only trying to distract his passengers from the storm and lift their spirits. I was too sick to care one way or another, feeling that I would never live to see land again.

The *Serpa Pinto* had drifted off course during the storm, and, after two

45   The Spanish Civil War began in 1936, in the aftermath of a rebellion led by Generalissimo Francisco Franco against the Republican government. It ended in 1939 with the defeat of the Republican forces and the establishment of a totalitarian regime by Franco. The war is described as a "general rehearsal" for the Second World War, in which Spain was neutral.

weeks at sea, we found ourselves along the coast of Florida. The ship corrected its course and headed back north to New York Harbor, which we reached on January 9, 1941, eleven months before Japan attacked the U.S.A. at Pearl Harbor.[46] As we approached the harbor, everyone went on deck, straining to get a glimpse of the Statue of Liberty, but, as it was a foggy day, we could only see a vague outline. We had finally arrived at our long-awaited destination, "land of the free and the home of the brave." The best thing about our long ordeal was that our family had remained together. As I peered through the fog at the Statue of Liberty, I wondered what life in the U.S.A. would have in store for me.

IN THE U.S.A. AT LAST

Two of my mother's sisters and a brother were waiting for us. I had never met Aunt Clara before. She went to the U.S.A. when she was sixteen years old and my mother had not seen her for twenty-eight years. I had only met Aunt Helen briefly when she stopped in Berlin en route to visiting her two brothers in Vienna in 1938. Uncle Paul was no stranger to me. He had visited us in Berlin several times, and once brought me a beautiful doll with real hair and eyes that moved from side to side. Tired and travel-worn, we were greeted rather formally; we had been expecting a warmer welcome.

We loaded our baggage into Uncle Paul's car, and were on our way to Aunt Clara's apartment in Brooklyn, where we would spend our first night in the U.S.A. I was surprised that no one suggested taking us to a hotel instead of to her tiny three-room apartment.

As soon as we were on our way, Uncle Paul started talking, painting a bleak picture of life in the U.S.A. This was not the first time we heard his pessimistic views. During our seven-month stay in Tangier, we received several disturbing letters from him, telling us to stay in North Africa as long as possible. As he described it, the opportunities for finding work in the U.S.A. were very bleak. The country was still in the aftermath of the Depression

---

46 Pearl Harbor is a bay in Hawaii where the American naval fleet maintained a large base. A Japanese surprise attack against the base on December 7, 1941, brought the U.S.A. into the war.

and some people became so desperate that they jumped out of windows. I remember how furious my mother was when she received those letters, when we were stranded in Tangier not knowing if or when we were ever going to get out of there. We had barely set foot on American soil, and Uncle Paul had the audacity to start his pessimistic ramblings again.

As her brother spoke, my mother leaned forward in her seat in the back, to be closer to her brother as he drove. While he described life in the U.S.A., my mother had to hold herself back from interrupting him. Finally, when she had an opportunity to speak, a tirade, which had been festering for months, poured out: "You must think we have been having a picnic traveling all over the world for a year and a half," she started. "You know we made it out of Poland by the skin of our teeth and had to leave Hella behind, which was a nightmare in itself. When we arrived in Italy and thought we were safe at last, Mussolini signed the Axis agreement with Hitler, and we faced the danger of being sent back to Poland. Through a miracle, HIAS got us passage aboard a ship to Tangier, or who knows what would have happened to us!" While my mother raised her voice, my father, brother, and I sat quietly, agreeing with her every word. "Perhaps you are worried," she continued, "that we are expecting financial help from you." I could see she was getting angrier and angrier. "Well, you needn't worry. We didn't need your help before and won't need it now. Don't you dare say another word to me," she threatened her brother. "You are lucky you're driving," she added, "or I might have…" she trailed off, not finishing the sentence. My mother's face flushed with the emotion she had held back for so long. Relieved of the anger she had been carrying around, she sat back in satisfaction. Uncle Paul did not say another word and drove in silence for the rest of the trip. I was glad that Aunt Clara and Aunt Helen had taken the train back to Brooklyn and did not have to witness that unpleasant scene.

The next day, we rented an apartment in Brooklyn, on Eastern Parkway, near Utica Avenue, just a few meters from Dubrow's Cafeteria. With the little English my mother had picked up, she convinced the manager of Dubrow's to hire her to work in food preparation. She also managed to secure a job there for my father: handing out tickets to customers at the entrance to the cafeteria. He had a limited knowledge of English, and this worked out well for him.

Willi was registered for his final year before graduation at Tilden High School. Through a family connection, he got a job as an usher at the Globe Theater in New York City, in the evenings and on weekends. With my mother, father, and Willi all earning money, I felt like thumbing my nose at Uncle Paul.

An acquaintance from Germany was attending Washington Irving High School, a girls' school, which, according to her, had a very strong art department. In view of my interest in art, she recommended that I consider going there. My mother was opposed to the idea of me taking any art courses, considering it to be a frivolous pursuit. I stood my ground, and she finally relented.

Because I had lost a year and a half while traveling from Europe and North Africa, I began school as a freshman at the age of fifteen. I took the afternoon sessions so that I could help out at home while my mother was working. My guidance counselor scheduled elocution classes for me to help me get rid of my accent and improve my language skills. There I met Elvira, my first friend in the U.S.A., an American of Italian heritage, and we hit it off from the start. A short while later, another girl, Doris, who was in our homeroom, joined us and we became a threesome, remaining friends until we graduated.

My family and I quickly adjusted to life in the U.S.A. After having lived in Germany under a dictatorship, I was continually amazed that anyone here could criticize any government authority, and even the President of the United States of America.

In the meantime, my father had acquired an inventory of men's clothing, and planned to open a retail store in New York City along the lines of the successful men's clothing store my parents operated in Berlin. They rented a store on Ninth Avenue and Fiftieth Street, near the old Madison Square Garden. The store was not far from Pier 92, so the Merchant Marines would be potential customers. Only when the store was fully stocked and ready for business did my parents feel comfortable giving up their jobs. We then moved to New York City to be closer to the store.

We had been in the U.S.A. for only eleven months when the Japanese attacked the U.S.A. at Pearl Harbor. The country was in shock, but the American people showed resilience and recovered quickly. Everyone pitched in with the war effort. In school, we were asked to knit little brown squares, which were later sewn together to make blankets and sent overseas to our boys in the service. People collected newspapers and tin cans. Young men and women enlisted and went to war, as did many actors and actresses. I remember hearing that Bob Hope went overseas to entertain the troops. Willi tried to enlist, but was rejected because of his birth defect — clubfoot — even though he had undergone corrective surgery at an early age. I tried to do my share by donating blood. I only dated occasionally because of the shortage of young men.

In 1943, with the war in full force, my mother's distant cousin, Helene, arrived from Belgium via North Africa. They knew each other from Tarnów, where they both lived when they were young girls, and had corresponded during the war. Shortly after Kristallnacht, we sent a large trunk filled with some of our important belongings to Brussels, where she was living at the time, which was later forwarded to us when we arrived in Italy. It included photographs of our cousins; I found myself looking at a young teenager who, unbeknownst to me then, was destined to become my husband.

A mutual aunt, Tante Lia, arranged for the two cousins to meet at her house in the Bronx. Tante Lia was one of my maternal grandmother's older sisters; she had immigrated to the U.S.A. much earlier, together with her sisters Welke and Basha. My mother asked me to come along to meet Helene, whom I had heard a lot about. When we arrived at Tante Lia's, my mother and Helene embraced and started speaking in Yiddish, the only language they both spoke fluently.

Helene brought Jack, the younger of her two sons, with her. He seemed to be a pleasant, somewhat talkative young man, with a great command of English. I was quite impressed, although I did not let on. We were sitting away from the others when Jack started telling me about the interesting job he had in Safi, Morocco, after the American forces landed in North Africa and liberated Morocco and Algeria.[47] A few days after the invasion, the Navy Shore Patrol hired Jack as an interpreter and translator. Fluent in French as well as in English, he did liaison work with the French police, assisting in various investigations. The chauffeur assigned to him drove him in a sidecar attached to a Harley-Davidson 500. It sounded like a very adventurous job for a young man in his late teens.

During our conversation, I found out that our paths had crossed when Jack and his family stopped in Tangier on their way to Casablanca, in the late

---

47   Northern Africa was the ground front where Britain fought Germany and Italy, after the Italian forces invaded, in late 1940, and the Wehrmacht joined them, in February 1941. The Allied forces landed in Morocco and Algeria, in 1942, for Operation Torch, and resumed the offensive in Tunisia, in April 1943. In May 1943, the Axis forces surrendered and 250,000 German and Italian soldiers became prisoners of war.

summer of 1940. Jack was going all out to impress me, but somehow I did not want to give him the satisfaction of succeeding. When he realized he was not gaining any points with me, he was annoyed, and, as he left, said sarcastically, "I understand that it's a leap year and girls can call boys, so why don't you give me a ring sometime." I was surprised by his remark and thought it rather obnoxious. I did not reply and we parted on a negative note.

* * *

After Willi graduated from Tilden High School, there was some talk about the possibility that he would continue his education and go on to college. He had always been a good student and considered studying pharmacology. However, watching my parents struggling economically, Willi felt that it was his duty to help them before pursuing his own career. My parents did not object when they heard about this, and, with his help, planned on opening a second store.

Before going ahead, my parents went to my mother's brother, Leo, to ask for advice. Uncle Leo had moved to the U.S.A. in 1939. He asked them how they would be able to manage two retail stores by themselves, and my mother then explained that Willi had offered to manage the store and postpone going to college. Leo agreed that it was a good plan. They no longer had any doubts, and opened another store. I wondered why Leo, who valued education above all else, did not insist that Willi should finish his education before going into business, as his own children had done.

The new store was located in a rough neighborhood. As newcomers, we did not realize how dangerous it was. At first, my parents took turns working with Willi there. Later, they hired part-time help so that he would not have to work alone.

A PREMONITION

In the summer of 1944, Willi and I went on separate vacations. The morning after he returned from his trip he walked into my room looking very upset. I was busy packing for my trip. I looked up at my brother and said, "What's the matter, Willi? You look awful." "I had a terrible dream last night," he said, rubbing his head. I stopped what I was doing and asked him what it was about. He took a deep breath, and tried to recall his dream. "There were these three black cats chasing a little white cat in a dark alley. Frightened, the little cat tried to run away, but, one by one, the three cats cornered the little cat. It hissed and clawed at them trying to defend itself, but to no avail... Slowly and deliberately, the three cats moved in on it and killed the helpless little cat." I could see the agony in Willi's face. "I don't know what to do," he said, his voice quivering, "I can't seem to get the dream out of my mind." Concerned, I sat down on the sofa next to him. I put my arm around his shoulder. "Willi," I said, "it's not like you to take a dream that seriously. You have to stop dwelling on it and remember that it was only a dream." "It's easy for you to say," he answered impatiently. "I saw it happen right before my eyes. I felt helpless, unable to save the little cat." "I know the dream seems very real to you now, but, before long, it will fade and you'll soon forget all about it." Willi nodded, still holding his head. I had to admit that the accursed dream affected me as well.

We sat together for a few more minutes, without saying anything, then he got up and took a deep breath. "You are right. I have to put that dream out of my mind and stop thinking about it. I had better go now," he said, still absorbed in his thoughts. Then he left without saying goodbye. It was the last time I saw my brother.

THE TRAGEDY OF A BROKEN DREAM

On Saturday, July 15, 1944, after Willi returned from his own week-long vacation, his part-time helper did not show up for work and my brother was alone in the store. Late that afternoon, just before Willi was going to close the store, three young hoodlums walked in and held him up. At first, he managed to fight them off and get to the phone. However, the thugs recovered, cornered him, and one of them fatally stabbed him.

* * *

I had already left for my own vacation at a hotel in the Catskills with two friends, Sarah and Erna, and the horrific events of the previous day were unknown to me. On Sunday morning, July 16, 1944, I was surprised when

Sarah's sister, Hannah, unexpectedly appeared at the hotel. My parents sent her to tell me that my brother had been in an accident and asked me to come home. Hannah would not disclose any additional information to me except that my brother was in hospital. I hurriedly packed my things, and Hannah and I took the next bus back to New York. I did not know what to make of the situation, but I remember having a sick feeling in the pit of my stomach. I tried to tell myself that it might not be as bad as it seemed, but could not get rid of that feeling. Hannah told me to go to Aunt Basha, my maternal grandmother's youngest sister, who lived in Brooklyn, where my parents would be waiting for me. I could not understand why my parents did not ask to meet me at the hospital.

When I went into the apartment, I remember thinking that it looked as if my parents were sitting *shiva,* as they seemed to be praying and crying at the same time. Sitting on the customary low stools reserved for mourners, they were oblivious to what was going on around them. I dismissed what I saw because I had not actually been told that Willi was dead. My parents did not get up to greet me. I remember trying to say something to comfort them, but they barely looked in my direction. Feeling almost like an intruder, I drifted into another room, where I sat down near a window and prayed for my brother's recovery. Suddenly, my Aunt Helen walked determinedly over to me and said, "I can't take it anymore. They are not telling you the truth. Willi was killed last night."

I stood up and gasped in shock, then sank back into the chair. I was unable to absorb what my aunt had said. I could not believe that my brother was gone, torn away from us, after all we had gone through.

There was no one I could turn to for comfort. My parents were grieving themselves, and did not comfort me or involve me in their suffering. I felt totally alone. I cried constantly for weeks, and was unable to keep any food down.

My poor father suffered in silence, and I would often find him crying in another room. In her grief, my mother turned against me. She tried to blame me for my brother's death, saying, "If only you would have gone on vacation with Willi, instead of with your friends, he might have lived." My parents, so absorbed in their own grief, were unaware of how deeply the loss was affecting me. I could not grieve openly, and tried to cover up my pain for my parents' sake.

* * *

The three teenagers who murdered my brother were caught several months later. In the trial that followed, we found out what had actually happened in the store that afternoon. Unfortunately, according to the law at that time, the sentence was less severe if the perpetrators' intent was to rob and not to kill. As it turned out, two of the three thugs were under age, and so only the eighteen-year-old was given a one-year sentence at Elmira Prison in upstate New York, and the other two were sent to a correctional facility for three months.

* * *

I knew that my mother always had a fascination with fortune-tellers and their ability to predict the future. Only after Willi was killed did she reveal to me that she had gone to see one shortly before we left Poland for Germany. My mother was anxious to know what the future held in store for her, as she was embarking on a new chapter in her life. "After the fortune-teller looked at my palm, she made her prediction. 'Many years from now, you will cross two oceans. The first one will only be a short voyage. The second one will be a long one and will take you to your permanent destination.'" Then, the fortune-teller hesitated, trying to find a gentle way to tell my mother what she foresaw. "'There, you will face a great tragedy.' 'A tragedy?' I repeated. 'What kind of tragedy?' I asked again, stunned by what I had just heard. The fortune-teller looked up at me, and said, 'I can't tell you what I saw. Even if I do, there is nothing you can do to change your destiny.'" Shaken by what she had heard, my mother paid her, noticing tears in the woman's eyes as she bade my mother farewell.

"I put the prediction out of my mind," my mother continued, "but after Willi's death, I remembered it. I'm glad that the fortune-teller didn't tell me the nature of the tragedy. Had I known, it would have been very difficult for me to live with it." My mother's voice broke as she tried to fight back her tears. Living through the tragedy changed my mother forever. I hoped that our shared grief would bring the two of us closer together, but for reasons I do not understand, it never did.

Although my memory of Willi has faded over the years, not a day goes by when I do not think of him. He was my big brother and protector, and whenever we were together, I always felt safe, as if nothing bad could ever happen to me. Willi never thought of me as his pesky little sister who tagged after him. On the contrary, he often asked me to come and watch him play in his table tennis tournaments. Also an ardent soccer enthusiast, he was his team's goalie. I remember watching him play often.

Willi knew how much I liked reading adventure stories, so he traded with his friends and brought books home for me to read. What I treasured most about him was that he taught me the important daily Hebrew prayer, the *Sh'ma*. He made me recite it over and over again until I knew it by heart, and only then did he trust me to say it by myself. It became such a habit with me that, unless I said the *Sh'ma*, I could not fall asleep.

Long after Willi was gone, his spirit remained with me. His death left me feeling desolate. I felt abandoned until Jack came into my life and helped to bring me back into the world of the living.

Fanny and Jack

Fanny and Willi

AFTER WILLI

The hot oppressive summer days following my brother's death dragged on without any relief in sight. *Shiva* for him was over, and our store was reopened. Both my parents were still lost in their grief, and it was hard for them to fall back into a routine.

To add to our grief, *shiva* ended on Willi's birthday, and instead of celebrating it, we were mourning his death. It seemed as if we had fallen into a bottomless pit out of which we were unable to lift ourselves. We hardly spoke amongst ourselves and moved about like restless ghosts. Willi's death had left us feeling hopeless, and nothing seemed to matter anymore.

In his grief, my father had become uncommunicative. After eating his meals with us, he would withdraw into another room. I would often find him sitting in his chair sobbing silently, holding a photograph of my brother.

My mother's response was unlike my father's. She became belligerent and argumentative, taking out her pain on my father and me. To protect himself from her tirades, my father would leave the room or quietly walk out of the house. Over and over again she would say, "What good is it to have escaped from Germany, only to come to the U.S.A. and lose our son? Surely, Willi's death is my punishment for not helping my sister." She tortured herself with these thoughts. Perhaps it was better that she expressed her grief, rather than suffer in silence.

She rejected all my efforts to console or comfort her, and, after a while, I stopped trying. I hoped that things would get better for her with time, but they never did.

At first, we tried to find some comfort by visiting my brother's grave. Every Sunday morning, we would take two trains from New York City to Queens, and then a bus from Jamaica to the Montefiore Cemetery, where my brother was buried. As we soon found out, those weekly visits to the cemetery did not make us feel any better, but only added to our pain. After a few weeks, it all became too much for my father. He could not face reliving the tragedy of losing his son, week after week, and had to stop going to the cemetery with us. As long as my mother wanted to continue, I went with her. I promised myself never to let her go alone, and I never did. I could not wait for the summer to end so that I could go back to school and get out of the house, where the atmosphere had become unbearable.

WE MEET AGAIN

W e were still at war when Jack, the cousin I had met a year ago, came back into my life. It could not have happened at a better time. He seemed to have appeared out of the blue, walking into our store in his white Navy uniform looking lean and fit. He said he happened to be in town and thought he would stop by and say hello. He briefly mentioned that he had heard about our tragedy and extended his condolences in a sympathetic yet congenial manner.

Later, when we were alone, Jack told me how he had come to think of me. "I was washing the deck of the USS *Texas* battleship when we were docked in Sicily. I heard a message coming over the megaphone, 'Fanny, come alongside.' It was a code word for that day. Something clicked in my head and I remembered the cousin I had met not too long ago. It was like a subconscious message and I made a mental note to look you up. Four weeks later, we headed back to Brooklyn Navy Yard, and here I am."

Although somewhat skeptical when I first heard the story, Jack sounded so genuine that I believed him. He seemed much more reserved and less forward than I remembered him. Seeing him with fresh eyes, I could not explain my reaction to him the first time we met. Actually, Jack was quite appealing with his curly red hair and ruddy complexion. There was also a twinkle in his eyes, reflecting a streak of mischievousness.

"You don't seem to be quite as sure of yourself as when we first met," I could not help saying. But Jack just smiled. He was not about to have another disagreement with me. Jack later confessed that he had been so taken with me when we first met he did not know what to do to win me over. "I tried so hard to impress you, and when it did not work, I became frustrated and messed up. By then I figured you'd never want to see me again. Let's forget about what happened and start all over," he suggested, and then asked me out on a date. I accepted and was actually looking forward to seeing him again.

After Jack left, the sultry weather suddenly turned into a torrential storm. I hoped that he made it safely to the subway. I stood watching the storm through our store's glass door. The streaming rain, like arrows, hit the pavement. Blinding lightening zigzagged through the sky, followed by rumbling thunder. Somehow, the rain seemed to wash away some of the sadness I had been feeling for so long. When the sun finally broke through the clouds, it was like a promise of better times to come.

We met the following Sunday. It was a beautiful summer day, so we decided to go to Central Park, where we would be able to enjoy the outdoors and get to know each another at the same time. We walked side by side, inhaling the fragrance of the freshly-cut grass, not saying much at first. When we saw a bicycle rental place, we decided to rent a pair. I started out on my bike first, with Jack following close behind. "I'll race you," I said, and sped down the path, exhilarated, my hair blowing in the breeze. I had not felt so good in a long time.

When we got tired, we put our bikes down on the grass, and sat down under a tree to catch our breath. "Now is your chance to tell me about yourself," I said. "Where should I begin?" Jack said, trying to collect his thoughts. "I've been in the Navy for over a year now. I chose it because I worked for them before, as a civilian in North Africa." "That's right," I said, "you told me about it when we first met." "You know I have an older brother? His name is Eddie and he is in the Army serving in Europe." "I'd like to know more about the time you lived in Belgium," I said. "Where did you go to school?" "I attended the Lycee in Brussels and only had six months to go before graduating when the war began. I studied Latin for six years and Greek for five years as well as German and English." "Wow," I said. "I forgot to tell you that I play the violin," Jack added, "I began studying it at the Conservatory when I was ten years old. Unfortunately, I have not touched my violin since I joined the Navy and am concerned about getting back to it after such a long time." "I'd like to hear you play sometime," I said. "I will be happy to," he replied.

As we exchanged our views about life, we found out that we had a lot in common. Both of us were idealistic and shared similar moral values. Distantly related, we also came from similar backgrounds: Jack was raised in Belgium, and I grew up in Germany. Both of our families escaped from Europe during Hitler's regime and both of us also ended up in Morocco: Jack and his family had lived for over two years in Mogador, south of Casablanca. "There was not much for me to do there, so I played the violin to my heart's content, and also gave violin lessons to earn some money," he said.

At the end of the day we were holding hands. I expected Jack to kiss me, but he held off, and this puzzled me. I thought it very unusual for a guy who was so sure of himself. However, he asked me to wait for him, and not date anyone else while he was away. I was totally taken by surprise and answered, "Don't you think we should get to know each other a little better?" Nevertheless, to my own surprise, I said I would wait for him.

Jack finally kissed me after our second date and explained to me later that he did not want to rush me, fearing rejection after the hard time I gave him when we first met. He also told me about some of his experiences in the Navy. He really had the gift of gab and knew how to make me laugh, something I had not done much since my brother's death. We seemed to be in perfect harmony as we talked and exchanged ideas.

"Now it's your turn to tell me about your stay in North Africa," Jack said. "As you know," I started, "we spent seven months in Tangier. It was the first time I had ever seen the ocean and the beach. If it had not been for the uncertainty of the war, our stay in Tangier would have been like a vacation. I went to the beach almost every day with my friend, Rutie, who was also from our refugee group. Since I did not speak French, I could not attend school. Sometimes I babysat to earn some spending money I used for going to the movies." Then I told Jack about our escape from Poland and my mother's courage in saving our family.

"Funny that you should say that," Jack intercepted, "my mother also played an important part in making the decision for us to leave Belgium. France was already occupied by the Germans, and we knew that Belgium would be next. My father, who was in the wholesale produce business, expected a payment for a shipment he had made and did not want to leave before he got paid. 'Okay,' my mother said, 'you stay and wait to get paid. I am leaving with the boys tomorrow.' When he realized that her mind was made up, he agreed to leave with us. We packed our belongings into our car and the trailer we bought for the trip and left the next day. The road was packed with people in cars, like we were, or in horse-drawn wagons, or on foot. The strangest thing I remember was seeing elderly people in wheelbarrows being pushed by their children. At sundown on Friday, my mother asked my father to pull over. 'We are not going further until the Sabbath is over,' she said. She asked me to get the candles and a potato from our supplies. 'Cut the potato in half and make holes for the candles.' Then, she covered her head, lit the candles, and recited the blessing over the Sabbath candles. We had something to eat, stayed in our car, and listened to the radio."

"After the Sabbath was over, we started out again. The road was less congested and we were able to move much faster. We had driven a good distance when we met some people who told us that on Friday evening German airplanes bombed the road and people had been killed. It was a good thing we stopped, or I would not be here telling you about it now." Then, while I sat fascinated, Jack told me about their journey to Casablanca.

* * *

When Jack first walked into our store, it was only a few weeks after he had returned from overseas, where he had taken part in the Normandy invasion. He was an ammunition loader on the USS *Texas* battleship, and while lifting 200 bags of TNT, each weighing 103 pounds, he tore his abdominal muscles. He was given extended leave to convalesce after surgery for this.

His leave came at a very opportune moment. We saw each other during the week, as well as on weekends. We went to concerts and saw the latest Broadway shows, or we would just sit and talk endlessly about nothing. In no time at all, we were able to guess each other's innermost thoughts, and avoided thinking of the possibility that we could be separated at any time.

After he recovered from his surgery and his leave was over, Jack received orders to report to the USS *Henry R. Kenyon*, a destroyer's escort docked at the submarine base in New London, Connecticut. The ship had orders to head for North Africa to escort a French submarine that had been repaired there. Shortly after returning from North Africa, the USS *Henry R. Kenyon* was ordered to proceed to the Pacific Ocean theater via the Panama Canal. He was assigned to heavy physical labor, and refused to comply. Threatened with charges of disobeying an order, and since the captain could not see him, he was referred to the executive officer to explain the situation. He explained that he refused because his incision had not healed and the heavy labor might open it up. After going over his service record, the officer noted that Jack had worked as a civilian for the Navy in North Africa as an interpreter, since he was fluent in French, and did not understand why he had ended up as a seaman instead of a commissioned officer. He asked Jack if he would like to work with him in the ship's office as a yeoman. Jack agreed and was promoted to a third-class yeoman.

When Jack was overseas, we wrote to each other every day. It was the only way to keep track of what each of us was doing. I was sure that by now my mother was aware we had become serious about each other. When I told her that Jack and I planned to get engaged as soon as he was discharged, she stared at me in surprise as if this was the most shocking news. "You are going to get engaged? When did all this come about?" she asked. "It did not happen suddenly. Jack and I have been seeing each other for over a year, and, while he was overseas, we wrote to each other regularly. Why is this such a surprise to you?" I said. "Well, I thought you were friends and enjoying each other's company," she stammered, "but I certainly did not expect you to get engaged."

When my mother recovered from what she had just heard, she went into a tirade, telling me I was much too young to commit myself to one person and should give myself a chance to meet other young men before making up my mind. I told her in no uncertain terms that I was not interested in meeting anyone else and that Jack and I were meant for each other. But my mother paid no attention to what I was saying, and finally said it was her duty, as my mother, to stop me from making a terrible mistake. She insisted that I write to Jack and tell him that I needed more time. I told her that I could not write something untrue, but the more I resisted, the more she insisted I write to him. This went on for weeks and my mother would not let up. I could not concentrate on my schoolwork, and my stomach started acting up again. In the end, I gave in and wrote to Jack and said, as sensitively as I could, that, for the time being, we should put our relationship on hold and wait to see how we felt about each other when he got back. The truth was that I really had no choice. I knew only too well that if I did not comply with my mother's wishes she would take matters into her own hands, and there would be no telling how far she would go to break us up. I had to avoid that at all cost, or there would be no chance for another reconciliation between Jack and me.

While I was anxiously waiting for a reply from Jack to my "Dear John" letter, I received several letters from him, telling me what had been happening to him in the past few weeks. "Our ship, the USS *Henry R. Kenyon*, received orders to patrol the South China Sea, and, on this mission, we were attacked by low-diving kamikazes. Fortunately, no one was hurt and the ship escaped serious damage." I breathed a sigh of relief when I heard how he and his crew had escaped this dangerous attack. "But that was not all that happened. We were in the Philippines when we were informed by radio that the war was officially over, and the second atomic bomb had been dropped on Nagasaki. The war may have been over, but not for us! As our ship began its long voyage west, we were caught in the tail end of a typhoon, which, in its fury, ripped off all our lifeboats and we also lost one of our two propellers. Our ship, swaying at a sixty-degree angle through mountainous waves, almost capsized. Like Jonah when he refused to go to Nineveh to save his people from destruction, I felt I was caught in a storm that was life threatening. I was the only Jewish sailor on our ship, but was sure I had done nothing to arouse the Creator's wrath. I had to convince myself that this storm was a natural phenomenon, and that I had nothing to do with it."

"At about two in the morning, while I was in the radio room, we received a coded message which read, 'Proceed with extreme caution, you have just drifted into a floating minefield.' Stunned to hear this, we were all sure we were done for. The ship and its crew were like sitting ducks, and could have been blown into bits at any moment. There was nothing we could do except pray, and oh, how we prayed. At six in the morning, our captain asked for volunteer sharpshooters to try blow up some of the mines, but he realized it would be impossible to detonate the mines unless the bullet hit the pin. No one could possibly aim so accurately on a swaying ship. We do not know how, but we reached Yokosuka Bay. As the boat limped into the bay with only one working propeller, we were shocked to see the devastation around us and knew we would be stuck at the naval base for at least a week until the replacement for our missing propeller arrived. Since we were told that the food on shore was contaminated, we only ate what we had in our reserves. We then found out that the Japanese had cut loose the floating mines protecting Tokyo Harbor while at the same time surrendering to the U.S.A. aboard the USS *Missouri* battleship. We could not wait to get out of the Bay, and, as soon as we received the propeller and our ship was repaired, we were finally on our way home. We slowly crossed the Pacific, heading toward San Diego. We could not believe that the war was really over, and we would soon be on American soil, 'land of the free and the home of the brave', again."

After I read Jack's hair-raising account of what he had gone through, I thought that it was truly a miracle that they had all survived. But, my "Dear John" letter was on its way, and how I wished that I had never sent it. Jack did not deserve it, and I could not sleep, worrying about how much it would hurt him.

I was furious with my mother and blamed her for making me do it, but I was also angry at myself for doing something against my better judgment. I told my mother to stop meddling in my affairs. I only hoped Jack would accept my apology. When she saw how determined I was, my mother finally backed off and stopped interfering.

A few weeks later, I received the long-awaited answer to my letter. My hands were shaking as I tore open the envelope. "Dear Fanny" the letter began. "I know you were waiting to hear from me, but I needed some time to think about what you wrote. All I can say is that your letter did not sound like you. I suspect that your mother had something to do with it. I am on my way home and should be arriving in New York in a few days. I would like to see you and hope that we can work things out." "Thank God," I said to myself, "not all is lost after all."

The days passed slowly as I waited for Jack's call to tell me he had arrived. When I finally got the call that he was on the way to see me, I was so nervous that I could hardly contain myself. When the doorbell rang, my heart skipped a beat, and when I opened the door, we flew into each other's arms, as if nothing had come between us. We were together again, and that was all that mattered!

* * *

When I returned to school, I did not tell my friends that my brother had died. It was the only way I could temporarily escape the pain of it all. That year, I was elected to represent my class on the student council, and I felt good that my class had found me worthy of their votes.

As a senior, I had to make a decision about my future and hoped to pursue studies in Fine Arts, but my mother was opposed to this. She believed that such a career was a frivolous pursuit and would not be financially viable. My father did not want to get involved and left the decision up to her. The choices she gave me were either secretarial or fashion design school, which also offered pattern-making and sewing. "If you know how to sew," she reiterated, "you will always be able to make a living. And if worst comes to worst, you can always do alterations at home." I understood where my mother was coming from, but was very disappointed that she did not have any faith in my ability to become more than a seamstress. I was also angry that my mother disregarded my wishes and dreams for the future. Since I was financially dependent on my parents, I had no choice but to settle for what I was offered. After graduating from high school, I registered at the McDowell School of Design in New York City.

THE WAR IN EUROPE FINALLY COMES TO AN END

In 1945, the war in Europe was finally over. Hitler was found dead in his bunker in Berlin[48] and one could almost hear a sigh of relief sweeping through the world.

We realized that we could now look for our loved ones left behind. The Red Cross made available to family members a list of victims killed in concentration camps. On the day the lists were released, my mother was the first one in line. Anxious to see if anyone in her family had survived, she feverishly scanned through the names hoping against hope that no one from her family would be on the list, and especially not her sister's name. But to her horror, it was there in black and white, obliterating all other names from her sight. Hella Schneebaum née Honig, Josef Schneebaum, and Salo Schneebaum were exterminated in Auschwitz in 1941. Later, she told me, "I had to lean against the wall to keep myself from sinking to the floor. I was paralyzed, unable to believe that my sister was really dead. It's all my fault," she said, her voice breaking, with tears welling up in her eyes. "At least I could have tried to get Hella out of Poland, but I was so involved in taking our own family out that I forgot about Hella. When she came to say goodbye to us and begged me not to leave without her, it was too late. Now, I will have to live with that guilt for the rest of my life," she said, sobbing uncontrollably.

"Mom," I said, trying to distract her, "Do you remember the names of any of our family members who were not on the list?" "Come to think of it, I remember seeing my brother, Norbert, and his wife, Malla listed, but not their daughter, Cesia," she said, wiping her eyes. "Mom," I said hopefully, "if Cesia's name was not on the list, might it mean that she is alive?" "It's possible," my mother answered, still absorbed in the grief of losing her sister.

---

48   Hitler and the Nazi Party's top leaders went into hiding in the command bunker, in Berlin, where Hitler wrote his political will. On April 30, 1945, Hitler and Eva Braun committed suicide, and their bodies were cremated at his behest.

"I know how badly you feel about Aunt Hella, but think of it: Cesia may be alive. Even if there is only a glimmer of hope, we must do everything in our power to find her." "You are right," my mother answered. "We'll start looking for her right away."

While we were trying to figure out a way to find Cesia, we received a letter from my father's youngest brother, Chaim. He and his wife, Sabina, and their daughter, Ruzia, had miraculously survived the war. We were thrilled to hear from them, but saddened that their son, Yanek, a young boy of seventeen, had not survived. As we read on, my uncle told us about the unfortunate circumstances leading to the loss of his son. "A farmer not far from Tarnów was willing to hide us in the attic of their house and care for us," he wrote. "The four of us — Sabina, Yanek, Ruzia, and I — lived in a small room, with only one window. One evening when the window was open to let in some fresh air, the smell of onions wafted up into our room from the field below. Yanek, unable to resist the smell, ran out to fetch some, but never returned. We suspect that he was caught by a soldier on patrol and taken into custody. When they questioned him he must have convinced the Nazis that he was wandering about on his own, and did not reveal our whereabouts. We can't let ourselves think what our poor son had to go through to save our lives," my uncle wrote, his sadness coming through in his letter.

When I thought about what happened to my cousin, I realized that both my brother and Yanek had died violent deaths, and there were no men left on my father's side to carry on the family name.

A SOLE SURVIVOR FROM THE ASHES

My mother continued corresponding with her brother-in-law. She told him that she believed her niece, Cesia Honig, was alive, since her name was not on the lists that we had checked of people who had perished in concentration camps. "We would like you to listen to what people are saying in Tarnów. Perhaps someone knows what happened to her," she wrote to him.

Several weeks later, we heard from my uncle again, with some promising news. A rumor circulated in town about a Jewish girl from Tarnów who had been hidden by a Polish couple, but no one knew her name, or where she was.

"I think we have come to a dead end," my mother said, discouraged. "If that girl is Cesia, there is no telling where she might be. For all we know, she might have ended up in Russia." "I don't know why you are saying that," I objected. "It's only a few months since the war ended and she might not have had a chance to register with the Red Cross."

A few weeks later when we checked at the Red Cross again, Cesia's name was listed as a survivor. I was ecstatic and could hardly contain myself. "I knew it!" I said jubilantly. "I had a feeling all along that she was alive, and that's why I did not want you to give up." Through the Red Cross Cesia learned that her Aunt Regina in the U.S.A. was looking for her. She immediately wrote to let us know that she was well and still living with the Polish couple that had hidden her throughout the war. "I can't tell you how grateful I am to these wonderful people. They treated me like their own daughter, sharing everything they had with me. Afraid to be found hiding a Jewish girl, they moved out of Tarnów, telling their new neighbors that I was their niece. They were willing to risk their lives for my sake. I am glad to hear that your brother-in-law, Chaim, is willing to take me to Antwerp with him, and wants me to stay with him until I can immigrate to the U.S.A. Before I leave Poland, I have decided to sell our house. I just can't leave the Myjkowskis without compensating them for what they did for me. Then, at least, I'll be able to leave Poland with a clear conscience."

Soon, we received another letter from Cesia, in which she told us that she had sold the house. "Imagine, when I knocked on the door of our house, the people who lived there recognized me and greeted me with 'We guess Hitler did not kill you, but don't think the house belongs to you anymore. It's ours now,' then slammed the door in my face! Of course I was able to prove that the house was legally mine. I sold it and gave the money to the Myjkowskis." Cesia then left with my uncle and his family for Belgium. She had to wait three more years there until she was able to immigrate to the U.S.A.

Over ten years passed until Cesia and I met again. I was already married to Jack and had a fifteen-month-old baby boy, named after my brother. When Cesia finally arrived in the U.S.A., she went to live with our Uncle Leo. His three children were already married and living away from home. Leo and his wife gave Cesia the love and attention of which she had been deprived for so long.

Cesia and I had only seen each other briefly a few times, and never had the opportunity to be alone together, when she called me one day and

Fanny with her son Billy at a reunion with Cesia in 1951

said, "I really need to talk to you." She sounded pensive, not her usual self. "Sure, whenever you want," I said. When we met again, it was very emotional for both of us. All the years we had been apart seemed to fall away, and we became the same inseparable cousins we had been so long ago. For a moment, I could not help recall the last three weeks we spent together in the summer of 1939. We thought that innocent time in our lives would never end. Little did we know, after we said our last goodbyes, that we might never see each other again, and, here we were, two young women together again after so many years. "The reason I wanted to see you is because I want to tell you what happened to me after you left Tarnów with your father. It will be hard for me to recall those terrible years in my life, so please, bear with me," Cesia said. Reaching for each other's hands, Cesia started telling me her story. "The day your father came to take you back to Kraków, my father decided, on the spur of the moment, to leave Poland and head east towards Russia. All he wanted was to get away from the Germans. We quickly packed bedding, food supplies, and clothing onto our wagon and left. I foolishly only packed my summer clothes, thinking we'd surely be back before the cold weather set in. When we arrived in Brezany,[49] occupied by the Russians, we were able to rent a small house where we stayed the rest of that summer and winter. We had to heat the house with wood since coal was not available. Since I did not have any warm clothes, I had to stay in bed the whole winter. My poor mother had to trudge through the snow to go to the library to get books for me to read or I would have surely gone stir crazy."

"As the Germans advanced to the East, the Russians gave us the choice of going further east into Russia or back to German-occupied Poland. My father chose to go back to Poland. When we returned to Tarnów, we found that our house had been assigned to another Jewish family by the Germans. With no place to go, we went to Grandfather's house. Perhaps we could stay with them, we thought. The house was occupied by family members, and they looked at us with solemn expressions as we first walked in. Aunt Hella was there with her husband, Josef, and their 12-year-old son, Salo. Grandfather's children from his marriage to Gittel were living there as well. His oldest daughter, Reshka, had come from Bielitz with her husband, Leo, and their two children, Samush and Sonia, seven- and five-years-old, respectively. Grandfather and Gittel's two single daughters, Neshka and Ida, were there as well. No one welcomed us, and no one smiled."

"At first Grandfather was reluctant to have us stay with him because we had been away from occupied Poland for almost a year, and had lived with the Russians, who were Germany's enemies. The Germans might suspect that we were spies. 'Someone in our family has to go to the German authorities

---

49   Brezany was a city in the Tarnopol district of Eastern Galicia, where Jews had been living since the sixteenth century. When the war began, it was occupied by the Red Army, and flooded by refugees from western Poland. In the summer of 1940, while many of them were transferred to the remote areas of Russia, only a few managed to find a livelihood there, and some of them returned to Poland. On July 7, 1941, the town was occupied by German military forces and annexed to the Generalgouvernement.

and vouch that you are part of our family,' Grandfather said. It was a very unpleasant situation and we felt as if we were intruding on our family. In the end, it was somehow resolved, and we ended up staying at Grandfather's, but not for long. We arrived in Tarnów just before the Germans sectioned off a part of town as a ghetto. Every Jewish family was assigned to share a house with another family. We had to share a house with a family of five: three teenage boys and their parents. All of us received working papers and were assigned to work in certain factories. My father had to work in a cement factory, my mother in a factory that made uniforms, and I was sent to a leather factory that manufactured saddles. Every day at six in the morning we were escorted to the factories where we worked, and returned to our homes in the evening. I don't remember how many months we worked until we heard rumors that people were being rounded up and sent to concentration camps. We knew that our days were numbered."

"When we were living in the ghetto,[50] I often looked over the fence and saw life going on as usual. I remember thinking, 'How did this all happen? We are not animals. It is only because we are Jews that we are locked into a cage and have to depend on our merciless captors.' The dreaded day arrived. The Jewish police went from house to house handing out papers to everyone. My mother and I got papers with a 'K' on them, which meant deportation. My father got one with an 'O,' which meant he would continue working at the cement factory. The people who got papers with a 'K' were told to pack their clothes, report the next day, and line up to go to the town square, where we would get further instructions. I cried the whole night, worrying what was going to happen to us. 'What did I do to deserve to die? I am only 14 years old. My life should not be ending; it should be beginning,' I said to myself."

"The next day, those with 'K' stamped on their papers lined up outside the ghetto. I started crying again. My mother tried to console me. 'Don't cry darling. You'll see everything will be all right,' she said, but I would not be

---

50 The *Judenrat* in Tarnów, established in early November 1939, was immediately ordered to keep the refugees housed and fed. On November 11, 1941, an *Aktion* took place in the city, in which 3,500 Jews were sent to the Bełżec death camp. In the second *Aktion* there, on June 15, 1942, some 10,000 Jews were sent to Bełżec, and others murdered in the city and buried in pits nearby. Only after this, on June 19, 1942, was the ghetto in Tarnów established.

comforted. In desperation, I started praying, 'Dear God, if you help me out of this predicament, I promise I'll do all kinds of charitable deeds and help unfortunate people. I will never forget what you did for me.' I knew it was too late. Even God could not stop the Germans from carrying out what they were determined to do. We were now moving slowly past a factory. Two teenage boys I knew from school were waiting at the door to report for work. They made eye contact with me. When the guard went to the other end of the line, the boys walked over to us. Without saying anything, one boy pulled me out of the line, the second boy went to my other side, and the three of us walked away. It happened so fast I did not know what was going on. There was no time to say goodbye to my mother, but I am sure she knew what was happening. I did not look back, and the three of us kept on walking until we were a safe distance away from the line. One boy whispered something to the other, but I could not hear what he was saying."

"We reached unfamiliar streets. I could not think about anything except where the boys were taking me. We approached a fenced-in area housing some pigs. One of the boys unlocked the gate, pushed me inside, and said, 'Stay here, and we will tell your father where you are.' He then locked the gate and left. I waited and waited for what seemed like a very long time. 'Why wasn't my father coming?' I wondered. The smell of the pigs was making me nauseous. Finally, my father came. He talked to me through the fence. He was uneasy. 'There is a lot of unrest in town. People are being arrested and I had to be very careful coming here. That's why it took me so long. You will have to stay here a while longer until things calm down. I have to get back to the factory. Meet me there later and we'll figure out what to do.'"

"Then he left. I was alone again and did not know what to do. I do not remember how long I waited at the pigsty, but the stench became unbearable. I tried to unlock the gate, but the lock was stuck. I was retching and could barely keep myself from vomiting. I had to get out of there, but how? The only way was to dig myself out. I frantically started digging under the fence with my bare hands since the soil was soft. I kept on digging until I made a hole big enough for me to crawl out through. There was no one around, and I carefully eased myself through the hole until, at last, I was on the other side of the fence. I was free. I stood up, and brushed myself off. I looked around, but felt disoriented, and did not know where I was. This part of town was completely unfamiliar to me. I waited a few minutes to get my bearings.

'Start walking, and eventually you'll get to a part of town you recognize, and then you'll find your way to Father's factory,' I said to myself. I don't know how, but after walking around a long time I finally found the factory. Completely out of breath, I went inside. My father saw me, and we stepped outside. I tried to tell him what happened. He said he knew, the boys had told him. As he was talking to me, my father was uneasy, anxiously looking around in case someone saw him. 'I think I know what you'll have to do. No one knows you got a 'K,' and were going to be deported. Somehow you have to get back to the house, sneak in with the shift returning from work, and, in the morning go back to the leather factory, as usual.' The plan sounded feasible, but I really did not want to leave my father. I started crying. 'Can't we hide somewhere together?' I begged. 'No,' my father said, 'it won't work. All the places where people are hiding out will eventually be raided, and, if they resist arrest, they will be shot. The Germans are merciless. We can't chance it, and, if I don't report to work, they will start looking for me. If they find you with me, you'll be killed too. Please darling, I love you, I want you to live. Go back to the leather factory, talk to Mr. Myjkowski, whom you said took a liking to you. Here, take this diamond ring, offer it to him, perhaps it will be an incentive for him to hide you.' I stopped crying, 'I guess you are right. Maybe that is the only way out.' 'I have to get back to work,' my father said, 'Be brave, Cesia darling. I know how hard it is for you, but it's much harder for me!' Then, he pulled me into his arms, hugged and kissed me, and disappeared behind the factory door."

"I never saw my father again," Cesia said almost inaudibly, and then she started to sob. I thought her heart would break and I could not help but cry with her. After we both released our emotions, I said gently, "Let's take a break. I'll make some tea, and then you can decide if you want to go on, or tell me the rest of the story another time." "No, no," she disagreed, "It has taken me so long to get around to telling you about what I went through, I'll never have enough courage to talk about it again. So let's have some tea and then I'll tell you the rest of it."

After we had tea and calmed down, Cesia continued her story: "I went back to the leather factory the next morning as my father told me. Mr. Myjkowski accepted my offer and was willing to hide me. As I realized later, they probably needed the money the ring would bring because they were very poor. That night, he took me home, and my life in hiding began."

"After Stephanie and Frank Myjkowski took me in, they lived in constant fear of someone finding out that they were hiding a Jewish girl. People who wanted to get on the good side of the Nazis often reported Polish people who were hiding Jews. So, the Myjkowski would not let me go outside and took my excrement to the outhouse themselves. If someone walked into the house unexpectedly, I would quickly get into the wardrobe in their bedroom, and stay there until they left."

"One day, a neighbor walked in without knocking and said to Mrs. Myjkowski, 'I know you are hiding a *Jiduwka* (Jewish girl). I have been watching your house and saw her through the window. I know the Germans will relish this bit of information. Let me check the rooms and see for myself,' he said, mockingly. Mrs. Myjkowski stood there helplessly, unable to stop the intruder, but hoped that I had overheard him and would get into the wardrobe before he would see me. But it was too late. I heard his footsteps approaching the room I was in. I had no time to open the door to the wardrobe, so I quickly hid at the side of the wardrobe. To my dismay, I forgot that there was a mirror hanging on the wall opposite to where I was standing, reflecting my terror-stricken face. For a split second, our eyes locked. Then, the man turned and walked out of the room and out of the house without saying a word."

"We were never reported, but after that incident the Myjkowskis decided to move away from Tarnów. It was just too risky, not knowing if or when someone might report us to the Nazis. We moved to Torun,[51] north of Tarnów, near Gdańsk, and set up house there. It was very difficult for Stephanie Myjkowski. She was not well and depended on me to do most of the housework. I learned how to cook and make the most out of the meager meat rations we received. Stephanie showed me how to make the meat go much further by adding bread and potatoes."

"At Christmas time, I made little rag dolls out of scraps of material, which I sold at a small profit. As word that I could sew got around, neighbors started to bring me their clothes for alterations. Once, a woman brought me a man's overcoat and asked me if I could cut it down and make a smaller coat out of it for her son. She offered me a lot of money and even though I had

---

51   A city near Tarnów on the banks of the Wisla River, established in the thirteenth century; was Copernicus' birthplace. During the war, the few Jews who lived there were sent to the Łódź ghetto.

no idea how to do it, I accepted her offer. 'I'll figure it out, it can't be that difficult,' I said to myself. As soon as she left, I opened all the seams of the coat, laid each part of the coat on the table, cut out a smaller coat according to a pattern I made out of newspaper, and then sewed the smaller coat together. I surprised myself by how well the coat turned out. The woman was very pleased with it, and I had some extra money to give to the Myjkowskis, who told the neighbors that I was their niece who had come to help in the house."

"The hardest part of living with a Christian family was to pretend that I was Catholic. I attended church regularly. I learned the Catechism, which I knew so well that the nuns made me stand in front of the class and recite it by heart. 'That's the way you should all be able to say it. Cesia says it perfectly!' the nuns said."

"I went back to school in Torun to complete my high school education. I was biding my time. The war had to end sometime. When the war finally ended, it was almost four years after I had gone to live with the Myjkowskis. I had to get back to Tarnów to find out if anyone from my family had survived. When I went back with Mr. Myjkowski, I registered at the Red Cross as a survivor, and you know the rest of the story."

Cesia looked exhausted. It had taken a lot out of her to tell me about what she had gone through. There were a lot of anecdotes she had left out, but I was not going to make her tell me any more.

However, there were some things I really wanted to know, and Cesia was the only person who could provide the answers. "When you returned to Tarnów after the war, did you find out what happened to our grandfather, and our aunts and uncles?" I asked her. "Of course I did. That was the main reason for going back there. I asked as many of our Polish neighbors as I could if they knew what happened to my family, and most of them were able to fill me in. At the end of the summer of 1941, when I left for Torun with the Myjkowkis, our family was still living at Grandfather's house, except for Aunt Hella, Uncle Josef, and Salo. They were the first family members deported to Auschwitz. From what I heard, Aunt Hella was resigned to her fate. After you all left Poland, she had no fight left in her. She was not as strong as your mother. She knew only too well that nothing would stop the Nazis from carrying out what they wanted to do."

"Before I left, all the family members at grandfather's house were reassigned to live with other people. Reshka, her husband Leo, and their two children were given special dispensation to live in their own quarters. Leo, a fine tailor, made uniforms for the Gestapo and was very useful to the Germans. They were the last ones to be deported, in late October 1944, when the Germans knew they were defeated, and orders were given to clean out all the Jews from Tarnów. One of our neighbors witnessed Grandfather's arrest. As she told me, when he received his deportation papers, he refused to follow the orders. He told the German soldier that there must be a mistake because he was the father-in-law of Leo Reck, who made uniforms for the Gestapo.

"The soldier tried to explain that there were no exceptions, and everybody who got deportation papers had to go. Grandfather refused to accept the orders and somehow managed to break away and start running. The soldier yelled, 'Halt!' but Grandfather kept on running. They shouted, 'Halt!' again, and when he did not stop, they shot him in the back." I gasped in shock at hearing how my dear grandfather, a pious man who would not punish his daughter for hitting his new wife, had met his death.

It took a while for me to recover from the news of my grandfather's death, but I wanted Cesia to go on and tell me if she knew anything else about any of our other relatives: "Did you hear about anyone else?" I asked hesitantly. "Yes, there is a terrible story about Kleine Rivka and her family. Apparently, when she and her five children got their deportation papers, her husband, Aaron, was at work. His family was sent away immediately, and when he came back from work in the evening, they were gone. He frantically ran to the railroad station and asked where the last deportation was sent, and demanded to be sent to the same destination. The Germans said he could not be sent unless he had children with him. In blind desperation, he ran back to the ghetto, picked up some children left behind by their parents who hoped they would somehow manage to survive, went back to the railroad station and got onto the next transport."

* * *

I had met Kleine Rivka again on my last visit to Poland. On the spur of the moment, Cesia and I decided to pay her a visit. My mother had told me a lot about Kleine Rivka, and I was eager to meet her. There was no way for us to inform her that we were coming. Cesia knew where she lived, and, since it was not far, we walked there. It was a Friday afternoon, and she had just finished washing her wooden floor. She was surprised to see us. She recognized Cesia, and asked her who I was. "This is Fanny, Regina's daughter. She is here on a visit." "Ah, Regina's daughter. How is your mother?" she asked in Yiddish with the kindest of smiles. "My mother is fine," I said, shaking her hand and returning the smile. "I heard so much about you, and wanted to meet you."

A little boy, four or five years old, stood behind his mother peering at us, wondering who we were. He had the biggest eyes I have ever seen, and I could not help thinking they had a tragic look about them. His mother told him in Polish that we were his cousins, and he continued staring at us.

"I was just getting ready for *Shabbos*," Kleine Rivka said apologetically. "I am sorry you missed my husband, Aaron. He just went out with our other children to get something I need. I would have liked you to meet him and the rest of my family. Perhaps you'll pay me a visit again another time. Say hello to your mother for me." Then we left. The visit really made an impression on me. Long afterward, I kept on recalling the little boy's haunting dark eyes, whose name I do not recall. Hearing about Kleine Rivka and her fate was devastating for me. I hardly knew her, yet I could not help putting myself in her place. There was no way of finding out whether Aaron ever met up with his family. I hope he did, even if it was only for a few minutes.

Kleine Rivka, her husband, and their five children were among thirty-eight members of our family who died at the hands of their cruel captors. We were never able to find out what happened to my father's oldest brother, Yossel, his wife, Perel, and their five children. They vanished from the face of the earth, as if they had never lived. My father's sister, Mindel, whom, as a child, I admonished for arguing with my paternal grandfather, her husband, and their four children also disappeared almost without a trace. We only found out that they all died at one of the death camps in Poland.

As soon as the war was over in Europe, my mother's brother, Leo, hired a lawyer to find out what happened to his youngest sister, Frieda, whom he brought to Vienna when she was nine years old. After the Anschluss,[52] Leo and his brother, Paul, managed to escape to England, where they waited until the Polish quota allowed them to immigrate to the U.S.A.

---

52   The political annexation of Austria by Hitler in 1938 to establish Nazi Germany domination there.

While in England, Leo corresponded with Frieda, who was still in Hungary. She was undecided as to whether she should try to leave Hungary while there was still time. Frieda had a substantial amount of money in a Swiss bank and would not have had any trouble managing financially if she had left Hungary. Unfortunately, Leo advised her not to leave, but rather to convert to Christianity, assuring her that this would guarantee her safety in Hungary. As it turned out, she was far from safe. After the Germans invaded Hungary in 1944 and found out that Frieda and her family had converted, they went after them with a vengeance as if they were criminals. They hunted them down in a convent where they were hiding and forced the nuns to hand the family over, and immediately sent them to be exterminated at Auschwitz.

I was devastated to hear about Aunt Frieda and her family's fate. I wondered if my cousins Georg and Franzie knew they were going to die in the darkest hour of their short lives. I hope with all my heart they did not know. It is my only consolation.

What evil passion drove thousands of German citizens to murder millions of innocent men, women, and children? Did they turn into murderous barbarians overnight? Were they the same people who gave us Mozart, Beethoven, Goethe, and Schiller? Would it not have been better for them to refuse to commit these heinous crimes, and die with honor, rather than live with the guilt and shame for the rest of their lives?

I cannot bear to hear the German language, in which I once loved to speak and recite. Now, I only hear the echoes of the death sentences decreed on their innocent victims. I do not believe I could ever set foot again on German soil that is soaked with the blood of the thirty-eight family members I once knew and loved.

To honor the memory of my loved ones and the millions of people who were so shamelessly murdered in the death camps, it is our moral obligation to keep this horrific chapter of our history alive so that such unspeakable atrocities against humanity will never happen again. One day, I hope that nations of the world will unite and eradicate prejudice forever. Only then will we be able to live in peace at last.

EPILOGUE

MY MOTHER'S FINAL TRIUMPH

D ifficult though it was, my parents continued working in their store after my brother's death. All their dreams for their son were shattered, and they struggled to move past this terrible tragedy. They did, however, manage to buy the building where their store was located. The immediate benefit was the additional income from twelve apartments, which seemed to be a profitable investment. Although my mother had no experience in managing real estate, she decided to handle it herself. She enjoyed this new venture, but, to her dismay, found her tenants to often be troublesome. To put off paying their rent on time they would deliberately break things in their apartments; subsequently, my mother hired a lawyer, and took them to court. Without investigating how the damage occurred and to expedite the cases, the judge would order my mother to repair the broken items, and give the tenant extra time to pay the rent, sometimes as long as two weeks.

My mother was annoyed at the judge's rash decisions, without giving her a chance to explain her side. In one case when the judge ruled in favor of her tenant, my mother could not contain herself. Furious at the judge, she jumped up from her seat, pointed her cane at the judge and shouted, "You Hitler!" Shocked at this, the judge banged his gavel on his desk and angrily declared, "You are in contempt of court, come and see me in my chambers!"

Upset by the judge's reaction, my mother went pale, and told my son, who was sitting next to her, that she was not feeling well. Concerned about his grandmother, who was well into her eighties, he told her to stay put. He would go to see her lawyer and explain the situation to him. When my mother's lawyer heard that she was not feeling well, he advised my son to put her into a cab and send her home, and he would take care of the rest. Her lawyer explained to the judge that his client had taken ill and had to be sent home. Afraid of unforeseen repercussions, the judge dismissed the case. My mother was glad she did not have to face the judge and most likely have to apologize to him, if he ruled unfairly against her one time too many. Later, she bragged about her outburst in court: if nothing else, at least she had told the judge what she thought of him.

Regina, 1980

MY FATHER'S DEATH

When my parents were in their seventies they decided it was time for them to retire and spend their winters in Florida. They did so for several years, until my father's health began to fail. Suffering from congestive heart failure, he had a pacemaker installed to regulate his heartbeat. As his illness progressed, my parents stopped going to Florida and my mother hired a live-in caregiver for him.

In the spring of 1984, shortly after our first grandchild was born, my father had a mild heart attack, according to his doctor. He was hospitalized, and when we came to visit him the next day, he was sitting up in bed, attached to a monitor and an IV, looking quite well. His roommate struck up a conversation with us and told us that my father had a restless night, tossing and turning as if he was fighting someone off. During this conversation, my father seemed unaware that the man was talking about him. At first we were concerned, but later put it down to a bad dream.

To make sure my father was okay mentally, pointing to herself, my mother asked him in Yiddish, "Wer bin ich?"[53] Surprised by the question, he answered, "Die bist Psachye Honig's tochter."[54] "That's right," my mother answered, but I saw that it was not what she expected him to say. She was puzzled as to why he had referred to her as her father's daughter instead of his wife, Regina. Apparently, she did not realize that my father had been very proud to have married the daughter of the man he had greatly admired for so much of his life!

Shortly after we had returned from our visit at the hospital, we received a call from his doctor regretfully informing us that my father had suffered another heart attack, and passed away peacefully in his sleep. Both of us were shocked to hear the news, especially so soon after our visit when he seemed to be relatively well. He was eighty-eight years old.

We made the funeral arrangements as soon as possible, so as not to delay burying him. He was laid to rest in the Montefiore Cemetery, next to my brother's grave.

My mother found it hard to adjust to living alone after being married to my father for over sixty years. She missed my father's companionship, and

53   Who am I?
54   You are Psachye Honig's daughter.

relied on me more and more. She had a live-in caregiver, but expected me to be available at all times. When Jack and I occasionally had social obligations and could not accommodate her, she would say to me, "You can have many husbands in your life, but you only have one mother!" She expected me to be at her beck and call and made unreasonable demands, not taking into account that I had a husband and family to care for.

When she tried to reach me and my line was busy, she would ask the operator to interrupt my call, claiming it was an emergency. When she got through to me, she would tell me she was not feeling well and I should come over right away. I would drop whatever I was doing and drive frantically to her house expecting the worst. When I arrived, I would find my mother resting on the sofa in her living room.

"I am feeling better now," she would say with her eyes closed, to avoid seeing how upset I was. This happened many times, and I felt as if she was testing me to see if I would make myself available. These emergency calls would upset me so much that I would not be able to function for the rest of the day.

My mother, who had always been demanding, became even more difficult after my father died. I hoped that our relationship would eventually take off and we would become closer, but my mother never tried to understand what I was all about. She did not have any appreciation of my interest in art. She had always considered my artwork a waste of time, mainly because there were no immediate business prospects in it. She wanted for me what she wanted for herself: to be a successful businesswoman and make a great deal of money. She did not believe I could be happy as a stay-at-home mom raising my family.

When my children were still small and she came to visit and saw me buried under mountains of laundry that had to be folded, she would say unsympathetically, "If I were you I'd run away and no one would be able to find me." I derived a deep sense of satisfaction from caring for my family, a sentiment my mother did not share.

I well understand why my mother, having lived through two world wars, strove to become financially secure, and, when she finally succeeded, even though she would never admit it, did better than she ever expected.

MY MOTHER'S DEATH

When Jack sold his business and retired, we bought a condominium in Florida so we could spend our winters in a warmer climate. Our condominium was large enough to accommodate my mother and her caregiver, Jean, and we asked my mother to join us. She spent the first winter with us, but, after that, stayed in an assisted-living facility. She did this for several years until the winter of 1993. She was approaching her ninety-fifth birthday when she decided not to come to Florida any more. "In case something happens to me," she said, "I don't want to be sent back in a body bag!" It was a rather blunt way of putting it, but she had a point, and I did not insist that she change her mind. I felt she knew what was best for her. That winter, she stayed at home and we kept in close touch. Jean was with her at all times and our son, Bill, who lived only minutes away, looked in on her every day.

A few weeks after my mother had celebrated her ninety-fifth birthday at the home of our son, Marc, she called Bill and told him she might have caught a cold and wanted him to take her to the doctor to be checked out. The doctor assured her that all was well and sent her home. A few days later, Bill called and told me that my mother was not herself. "She is sleeping a lot and I have the feeling that she wants to see you." I did not like the sound of it, and immediately booked a flight to New York. I arrived the next day and went directly from the airport to my mother's house. Jean opened the door and said, "Your mother has been waiting for you, but she may be asleep." I walked quietly up the stairs and tiptoed into her room. My mother was sound asleep. I sat down on a chair beside her bed and waited for her to wake up. I looked at her face and saw that she was at peace. She must have sensed that I was in the room because, within a few minutes, she woke up. When she saw me, her face brightened, "Ah, my child," she said, "you have come." Then, she closed her eyes and went back to sleep. Thus, in her final moments, she had finally acknowledged me as her child. I had been waiting to hear her say those words almost my entire life, and at that moment she finally became the mother I had always wished for. Surrounded by her family and friends, we put my mother to rest next to her husband and son. At last, she was at peace with herself and the world.

Despite the tragedy in her life, my mother had been lucky in many ways. She had four grandchildren, whose lives she was very much a part of: two boys,

Bill and Marc, and, two girls, Cheryl and Janet. She attended the weddings of all four of her grandchildren, and lived to see six great-grandchildren come into the world, and two great-grandsons, who were born after she died, were both were named after her.

There is a famous saying in the Mishna, "He who saves one soul saves the entire world."[55] Saving her family was my mother's greatest accomplishment by far, for which her family will always remember her.

---

55   Mishna Sanhendrin, Chapter 4, 5.

POSTSCRIPT

Throughout my adult life, my thoughts would often return to the early years of my childhood and the carefree times I spent at the Auguststrasse Jewish school for girls in Berlin. The school was a refuge for me from the turmoil brewing around us.

Surprisingly, the teachers were able to create an atmosphere of stability, free of anxiety, during those turbulent times under Hitler's regime, while outside school many were aware of the seriousness of the political situation. The teachers were intent on making life as normal as possible and teaching their students as much as they could. As a student in the school, I found the daily routine comforting. Every morning, we started the day by singing in unison, to focus our attention on life in the classroom. During cold winter mornings, we were served hot chocolate, prepared by our teachers. I looked forward to going to school, and never wanted to miss a day. Most of all, I remember that the teachers instilled in us the importance of always being respectful and well-mannered, especially during those trying times.

Fraulein Lichtenstein, who was my teacher for four consecutive grade-school years, made a lasting impression on me and remained an influential force in my life. One day, she informed us that due to the increasingly difficult situation for Jews in Germany, she would be leaving to join her brother in the Land of Israel. Although saddened by the news, we bade her a fond farewell.

As the years went by, my desire to see my teacher grew stronger, and I wondered if there was a way to find her and meet her again. In 1974, my daughter, Cheryl, who was then seventeen years old, went to Israel on a work-study program. She stayed on Kibbutz Tirat Zvi for seven months. I thought this might be an opportunity to find my teacher. Cheryl made some inquiries and found it was much simpler than we had anticipated. She was advised to place an advertisement in a newspaper to which many immigrants from Germany subscribed. She received a reply from one of Fraulein Lichtenstein's former students, who told her that our teacher was alive and well, and gave her address in Haifa. Cheryl sent me the information. I was overjoyed and immediately shared the news with my husband. We cleared our calendar and made arrangements to go to Israel. I wrote to my teacher to tell her about our plan. She wrote back including the address of my dear friend Susie, which was an unexpected bonus, and I made plans to meet her too.

When we arrived in Israel, I contacted my teacher and arranged to meet her and her husband for lunch at the Dan Hotel in Haifa. I was nervous. Inside, I was still the little girl in awe of her teacher. I need not have worried. I recognized her immediately, we greeted each other warmly, and introductions were made all around. Since my German had become somewhat rusty, I spoke to her in English.

We talked about people we had known in Germany, and I told her about life in the U.S.A. I also told her about my daughters, Cheryl and Janet, who were with us at the time, and my two older sons, Bill and Marc, and my life as a stay-at-home mom. Jack took a photograph of all of us sitting around the table. It was hard to believe that this reunion with my teacher was actually taking place and I was pleased to have some proof of it.

The next day, we met again. Fraulein Lichtenstein invited us to lunch at her home. I rang the bell, and Fraulein Lichtenstein opened the door. We were greeted by a Beethoven overture, blending in with my teacher's welcoming voice, "If a former student wanted to see me after so many years, I must have done something right!" This was one of the most moving experiences I have ever had. When we reluctantly said goodbye, I sensed we would never meet again. I was right; we never did. But we continued to correspond for many years, until I was informed of her passing.

My long-awaited visit with Susie was extremely emotional for both of us. After hugging one another, we looked at each other in disbelief. Susie only said one word — *unglaublich* (unbelievable). With her winning smile and pretty face, she looked very much the way I remembered her.

We stayed at Kibbutz Ma'ayan Zvi, where Susie lived with her family. She reserved a room in the guesthouse for us. We met her family: her husband, Shlomo, and their three children, Erella, Eldat, and Orit, her youngest, who was the same age as my daughter Janet. We ate in the communal dining room, and sat around the pool. We chatted endlessly, trying to fill in the gaps from years of separation. I was curious about what happened to Susie after she left Berlin for Denmark. She started telling me her story. "Did you know that I was interviewed by Leon Uris's team while they were researching the background for his book *Exodus*? But they never included what happened to me.... The hardest part for me, and I am sure for many others, too, was leaving my parents. Even though I was leaving for Denmark with their blessing, I knew in my heart that it would be the last time I would see them. After I arrived in Denmark, I went to live with an elderly Jewish couple, who treated me like their own daughter. I was biding my time, anxiously waiting to leave for the Land of Israel and join my sister, Friedel, who was already living on Kibbutz Ma'ayan Zvi. The Danes soon realized the threat of the Nazi invasion was upon them. In response, Sweden unofficially opened its borders to the Jewish refugee children stranded in Denmark. Volunteers smuggled the children, including me, into Sweden by boat. When I arrived in Sweden, I was already a teenager and had the opportunity to take a nursing course. Shortly after I finished it, we heard that several ships were leaving from Sweden for Palestine via Marseilles. I got a place with one of the groups, which according to rumors, was organized by the *Hagana*."[56]

"During our journey, we were informed that Palestine was under the British Mandate. Our ship only got as far as Cyprus, where we were subsequently detained.[57] While stranded there, we ran out of food, water, and medical supplies. We had only taken sufficient supplies for the trip to the Land of Israel. There were hundreds of passengers aboard. Some were

56 The militia organized by the Jewish community in Palestine, before the establishment of the Israel Defense Forces. Founded in 1920, the *Hagana* organized the clandestine Jewish immigration (*Ha'apala*), in the 1930s.

57 Since the British Mandatory Government only allocated a few "certificates" (Palestine immigration visas), the *Bricha* (escape) movement in Europe was organized to bring Holocaust survivors to Palestine. The British stopped the *Ha'apala* vessels on the high seas, initially interning the passengers in Atlit, Palestine, and later in Cyprus, where they were held in detention camps until the establishment of the State of Israel.

survivors of concentration camps and in poor physical condition. Many women were pregnant, and some were about to give birth. I was one of only two people on board with any medical training. I suddenly found myself with all the responsibility for the passengers' physical welfare on my shoulders. Fortunately, I found a dentist on board who was willing to help. We struggled to keep the situation under control. With limited medical supplies, we were unable to help many of the passengers. The British were in no hurry to send us help, in the form of the medical supplies we so desperately needed, and so forth."

"Despite our best efforts, the seriously ill passengers began to die. Since, according to Jewish law, the dead had to be buried as soon as possible, the British permitted us to take the bodies to the mainland for burial. As a nurse, I was assigned to escort them ashore. Ironically, the beach happened to be guarded by Danish soldiers at the time. One day, while on such a mission, I overheard a soldier speaking in Danish, of which I knew a little. I turned to him and said, 'Some time ago, your country sheltered me from the Nazis while I was waiting to immigrate to the Land of Israel. I can't believe that you are helping the British to keep us out of our homeland.' Surprised to be addressed in his native tongue, the soldier apologized and tried to explain that he had to follow orders. However, he offered to make an exception and look the other way if I wanted to enter Palestine secretly. Outraged, I refused. 'Do you think I would abandon my people when they need me so desperately?' Then, I had an idea, and presented my plan, without hesitation. "There is something you can do to help. Many people on board have families in Palestine who are waiting to hear from them. They don't know we have been detained in Cyprus. They don't even know if we are dead or alive. Every time I come to escort a body ashore, I will bring you some letters from our passengers to their families. If you would mail them, you would be doing us a great service.' The guard agreed and was pleased he could do something for our passengers. When the restrictions were lifted and we were finally able to enter the Land of Israel, we ran down the gangplank, shouting with joy. Some people kissed the ground, others embraced one another, while others burst into song. There was no holding back the euphoria at finally entering the Land of Israel."

I was deeply affected by Susie's story and sensed it must have been important for her to share it, and, perhaps she hoped that through me, her story would live on. Susie and I had four more visits together: three in Israel and one in New York. Our last meeting was in 2007. It was deeply comforting for us to come full circle, and share the joy our families were bringing us.

Fanny with her husband Jack, children, and grandchildren at the Bar Mitzvah of grandson Alex Ganes in 2006, photograph by courtesy of Tony Maltese

Fanny with her children and grandchildren at the wedding of granddaughter Alyssa Lust in 2014, photograph by courtesy of Brian Marcus

ACKNOWLEDGEMENTS

For many years I told myself that someday I would write my family's story. My mother was a powerful force in my life; my memories of her, my father, and of my dear brother, Willi, as well as the family members I lost during the Holocaust, are recorded here so that they will live on.

I wish to thank my cousin Myrna Rose, who diligently and patiently typed the first draft of my story on the computer; Jean Irwin, Dana Kantrowitz, and Chelsea Seely for their keen deciphering skills in translating my writing to the printed word in the initial stages of this project; my daughter, Cheryl Harris, for her help in finding just the right words to express some of my thoughts; my daughter, Janet Lust Ganes, for contributing artwork inspired by my stories; my grandson, Jesse Ganes, for his technical assistance with the photographs; my grandson, Ilan Harris, and my granddaughter, Rebecca Harris, for their close reading and loving suggestions along the way. In addition, I am grateful to Dr. Bella Gutterman for her introduction. Finally, I want to express my deepest gratitude to the production editor Ita Shapiro Haber and the wonderful team at Yad Vashem Publications for their work on the book.

Sabbath Prayer

Rescued, photograph by courtesy of Monni Must

These are two of many stone sculptures that were created by the author over a twenty-year period, and represent significant moments in her life.